# A Different
# BEAUTIFUL

# COURTNEY WESTLAKE

**SHILOH RUN** PRESS
An Imprint of Barbour Publishing, Inc.

Cover image by Tara Long Photography.

Published in association with The Blythe Daniel Agency, P.O. Box 64197,
Colorado Springs, CO 80962-4197

Published by Shiloh Run Press, an imprint of Barbour Publishing, Inc., P.O.
Box 719, Uhrichsville, Ohio 44683, www.shilohrunpress.com

*Our mission is to publish and distribute inspirational products offering exceptional
value and biblical encouragement to the masses.*

Member of the
Evangelical Christian
Publishers Association

Printed in the United States of America.

# CONTENTS

# DEDICATION

To my husband, Evan, and two beautiful children,
Connor and Brenna: you have enriched my life
in more ways than I could ever describe.
I love you with all of my heart.

# INTRODUCTION

When we encounter the unexpected, one of the most commonly used phrases is, "My world was turned upside down."

But when my husband, my son, and I welcomed our daughter into our family, our world was not turned upside down.

When something is turned upside down, it falls apart. When it is upside down, it is destroyed and cannot be rebuilt. When liquid is upside down, it pours out, and you can't fill your cup back up. When a LEGO tower is turned upside down, the pieces fall off, crash, and break apart.

But not our world. Our world was shaken up. When you shake something, only the strongest pieces remain standing. The weak pieces fall to the wayside.

With the arrival of our daughter, our world was shaken to the core. But the strongest pieces remained—our marriage, our relationships with our family and our dear friends, our home, our jobs, and our community support. The most important priorities not only remained but grew stronger.

And through this, we came to realize how unimportant those weak pieces were that fell apart and fell off—pieces of our lives that were not priorities, that didn't matter.

With the strongest pieces remaining, we could focus on the important. With the unstable and nonessential pieces gone, we now had a clearer view of what was most important.

The clutter we kept adding to life as we busied ourselves with jobs, social activities, and other people suddenly gave way to a clarity we had never experienced before. Suddenly, the beauty of God was before us in the most raw and miraculous form.

Before our daughter was born, I wasn't truly living; I was only thinking about living.

But then she arrived on the scene, and life said, "Let's do this." She came into our lives and pushed us out into the wide-open space of a world that was waiting for us to appreciate and celebrate all of the beautiful it offers us on a daily basis, sometimes in moments we are least expecting.

# CHAPTER 1

## Pink Nail Polish

$\mathcal{I}$ sat my daughter, Brenna, up on her changing pad as I snapped up her outfit after a diaper change. And as she looked around, chattering, her eyes fell on my feet, with toenails painted in deep pink.

"Ow?" she asked, associating the color with blood and a hurt toe.

"No, not ow. Mommy put a pretty color of paint on my toenails," I explained as best I could in toddler language—also beginning to think that the concept of painting nails sounded a little ridiculous as I attempted to describe it.

I showed Brenna my nail polish bottle, and then, of course, she pointed to herself. "Me!" she exclaimed, and her underdeveloped speech made it sound more like "Neigh!"

I had never painted Brenna's nails before, though she was two and a half years old at the time. I had really never even *thought* about painting her nails.

Brenna's toenails are a product of a rare skin disorder she was born with, a diagnosis that came as a shock to everyone after a typical pregnancy; her nails grow in such a solid, thick yellow that there have been times we've had to trim them with side-cut pliers.

Like her skin, Brenna's nails grow way too fast—an effect of a mutated gene. This single mutated gene means the top layer of her skin has trouble doing its jobs.

And with her diagnosis at birth, there were some things that I, as her mother, realized might never happen—mother-daughter traditions I envisioned for months when I heard the ultrasound tech utter, "It's a girl," that seemed lost to the staggering severity of Brenna's life-threatening condition.

Things like putting on my daughter's makeup for school dances. Things like curling my daughter's hair for a family picture.

And, so I thought, things like getting our nails painted together.

I balked just for a second before courage set in. I could have said no. But my husband and I have decided we're not really in the business of saying no in the face of the unknown anymore. We'll have to tell Brenna no enough as it is, when her body simply won't allow for something. So we refuse to say no simply when we're nervous or scared.

I didn't know exactly how her nails—thick but sensitive—would react to polish. I worried about the polish getting on her skin and causing an adverse reaction.

But as her bright blue eyes begged me to open the bottle, I said enthusiastically, "Yes, let's paint your nails!"

As I carefully applied the pink color to her two big toenails, Brenna leaned over my arm, watching intently.

"Wow!" I exclaimed as I dabbed a final spot, waiting for her reaction.

"Wooo-ow," she whispered slowly.

Two brightly colored toenails, one on each foot. And the admiration that followed—the beaming as she held up her foot in the light that streamed in from the window.

The kind of admiration that made five minutes of painted toenails come to life in a celebration. I slowly realized the magic we were creating in those five minutes and in the moments that followed as she proudly showed off her pretty pink toes for the next week, extending her foot to nearly everyone she came in contact with.

Even if her toes were covered by socks, she knew how beautiful they were underneath, and she wanted to make sure everyone else knew, too.

It had nothing to do with the polish or the color. Rather, it was all about how she felt about herself. The way she felt as we painted together—loved and special. The way she felt around others—admired and engaged. Brenna felt beautiful because she was living in joy, in celebration, with those around her.

Since Brenna's birth, simple celebration is what we have discovered for ourselves, in and around some very hard parts of life. From the beginning, there have been what feels like endless doctors' appointments with more specialists than I have pairs of shoes.

Therapy sessions have packed our weeks so we can push Brenna to learn how to do the tasks that come so easily to other children—movements like pulling up on the couch, crawling, holding wide objects, and walking on different surfaces that are a whole lot more difficult when your skin doesn't flexibly stretch.

Simply enrolling in preschool instigated a multitude of meetings with nurses and administrators and therapists and teachers, along with health plans and other preparations, to ensure Brenna would be safe, healthy, and comfortable in the new school environment. And on the day I walked through those doors without her, I felt a bit helpless in my mommy heart, relinquishing Brenna's health routines to strangers and trusting them to care for her like I had for the last three years.

We have tried medication after medication just to see what might work.

We have had sleepless nights on end as she has gone through typical baby issues, like teething, on top of skin problems like uncontrollable itching. And she has endured hospitalizations when painful bacteria found its way into her skin.

In the whirlwind of four years, there have been so many kinds of things that you never expect to experience when you bring a child into the world or dream of times spent with her.

But with that has come a joy-filled life that we also never expected, the kind of overwhelming richness that is beyond comprehension when you have focused on washing tiny pink clothes in Dreft and making a list of what to pack in your hospital bag and stocking your freezer with post-baby meals.

Because even on the worst days, we can find beauty. Even when things don't look so wonderful, we can discover beauty somewhere.

Beauty extends from all pieces of our lives, just waiting to be noticed, to be appreciated, to be celebrated. And what our family has discovered after the birth of Brenna is that the best kind of beautiful—the truest beauty that God intentionally and lovingly created for us—is not only seen but also *felt*.

The most dazzling beauty in this world is not found in the magazines or even seen in the mirror. It is felt deep within our souls, and it is released to those around us in the forms of love, kindness, compassion, and generosity.

In a version of myself that I can hardly remember, I once believed beauty was something you strove for, something attainable that could be seen by everyone. But there is a different beautiful than the perfection our culture often worships.

That beautiful is found not when we open our eyes but rather when we open our hearts. That different beautiful is found in the uniqueness God has bestowed on every single one of us and the gifts He has placed within us to be shared with the world, if we choose to trust in Him and tell His story with our lives and our gifts.

Sometimes the most beautiful things even come from the unexpected parts of life that encourage us to search a little harder to find where the beauty lies—to put aside preconceived notions about what beautiful is and what it isn't and let the feelings of beautiful settle deep into our souls.

That is precisely the kind of beautiful, however, that brings into sharp focus the pieces of life that we may not otherwise celebrate.

Moments of kindness can get lost in the everyday rush. The opportunities to help our neighbor, to listen—*really listen*—to a dear friend, or to serve a stranger often pass us by as we wrap ourselves up in errands, to-do lists, and obligations.

How many times do we miss a chance to talk on a deeper level with our children because we are preoccupied with the next part of the day? How often do we notice people and make a snap judgment about them without opening our hearts to really getting to know more of their story? How often do we say no to using our God-given talents to enrich the lives of those who need help or those who are less fortunate because it feels too uncomfortable?

There is a whole new kind of beautiful to be discovered when we stop closing our eyes and our hearts to what is unfamiliar or unexpected. When we can focus on the goodness we are feeling rather than seeing, we can learn what it truly means to celebrate beauty in life—the joy, the passion, the deep relationships with each other and God, the dazzling, fleeting moments in front of us that might not otherwise cause us to pause.

Like painting with pink nail polish.

# CHAPTER 2

## Time to Meet Our Daughter

D o you think I should go?"

My husband, Evan, was scheduled to travel to Indianapolis with a colleague for business that morning, December 19, 2011, a Monday.

I had been having Braxton Hicks contractions for a few weeks, so even when the contractions moved down into my back and intensified that previous night, they weren't at all regular or persistent enough to cause either of us to believe our baby daughter was on her way. Our two-year-old son, Connor, had been induced a week late, and my labor was a long, intense process, so we were not expecting an early arrival, especially four weeks before my due date.

Evan rolled over that morning as his alarm clock sounded at 6:00 a.m. and asked how I was feeling.

"I slept on and off, and a couple of contractions did wake me up," I admitted. "But they're still so sporadic."

I told him it was probably fine to leave, and he ultimately decided to make the three-hour trip. He showered, loaded up his stack of bank papers, and headed out the door, making me promise to call him if anything changed. I followed suit with a shower, and I even took the time to curl my hair with hot rollers, thinking that if I was going to go into labor, I wanted to try to have a slight improvement over the beat-up look I sported in Connor's arrival photos. I had pushed for two long hours on my hands and knees, which left me swollen, with popped blood vessels on my face.

I turned on some videos for Connor and began to feel a bit of anxiety as I timed my continuing contractions, but they were still not regular at all. Emotions began spinning through my head with the thought that I might be holding my daughter in my arms soon. Excitement, worry, and nervousness swept through me, and I became so aware of my heart pounding quickly in my chest. . . Could this really happen today? I watched Connor for a couple of minutes, reflecting—as it seems common to do with the impending birth of a second child—on the fact that he was not going to be my only baby anymore.

I was not, however, feeling overwhelmed or overly anxious, the kind of overwhelmed you might usually feel as you debate whether you are truly in labor and what your next steps might need to be. Overwhelmed was at the top of my list of emotions with my firstborn's experience, so I was surprised to find a sense of calm to accompany my excitement, even as I considered the prospect of giving birth soon.

Eventually, I called my doctor's office and explained to the nurse what I was experiencing.

"It sounds like your body is trying to get ready for something!" she told me cheerfully.

She instructed me to head to the hospital if the contractions started coming regularly at about four minutes apart, so I called Evan and relayed this information to him.

A half hour later, I was making the bed when a contraction came on that was strong and intense enough that I had to lean against the bed to get more comfortable. I felt a huge amount of pressure, almost like I should start pushing, and I slowly made my way to the bathroom. I had just reached the bathroom tile when the pressure released, leaving me standing in a huge puddle.

For a split second, I was confused, and then it dawned on me: my water had just broken.

*Our baby would be born today.*

The fluid continued to stream out, giving me no choice but to awkwardly stride around my room with a towel between my legs, trying to remember what I should pack in my hospital bag. Evan was my first call as I informed him of this latest update—almost nervously giggling about the timing. At nineteen miles away from Indianapolis, he had to tell his colleague to make a U-turn at the upcoming gas station.

Connor wandered into the bathroom at that moment and pointed down to the growing puddle. "Mommy, clean it up."

My nervousness eased for a moment as I laughed at his two-year-old concern over the mess.

I quickly made calls to my mom and my mother-in-law, but they didn't answer. I panicked a little, forgetting when exactly I should go to the hospital after water breakage. I finally reached my dad, who headed over to our house to stay with Connor.

It was more than a little embarrassing to open the door for him, towel still between my legs.

"Sorry, Dad." I laughed, and he, looking everywhere but at me, told me to return to the bathroom and quit trying to pack. Thankfully, my dad deluged my mom with phone calls and finally was able to reach her and pull her out of a meeting.

Mom charged into the house as I was placing things into my hospital bag, pausing every so often for a contraction. With four weeks to go until my due date, packing a bag for the hospital was a check mark still waiting to be made on my birth list. The only thing that was folded in my black hospital bag was a tiny newborn sleeper I had picked out weeks earlier, which read "Daddy's Girl" among pink, green, and turquoise polka dots.

Though I was in active labor, I still felt the need to be as prepared as possible for an overnight stay, so I began shoving in T-shirts and sweatpants, deodorant and make-up, nursing pads and a pillow—as if no one could have brought me any of these things.

"We need to get going, honey," my mom insisted after a particularly strong contraction. "They're starting to come closer together, I think!" My mom seemed to be more observant of the timing of the contractions than I was, pulling me out of my need to control this surprise situation.

Twenty minutes later we reached the hospital, and after I got situated, I began asking for my epidural because I am not one of those women who wants anything to do with enduring more pain than I have to. And I knew from my prior birth experience that things can get pretty ugly pretty quickly.

Unfortunately, anesthesia was moving a little slow (aren't they always?), and I started clutching the hospital bed railings and trying to breathe like in the movies with every onset of a contraction.

When the doctor finally came, that enormous needle brought sweet relief, and the nurse checked my progress immediately following the epidural.

"Eight centimeters!" she declared, and I felt a tiny burst of pride that I had made it that far with no medicine; maybe I was not as much of a sissy as I thought.

With the comfort of an epidural, I updated my Facebook status from my iPhone: "In labor at the hospital. . . looks like we'll be getting an early Christmas present!" Friends began to leave comments of well wishes and "Can't wait to see photos!"

My own doctor, Dr. Brown, was not on duty at the hospital that day, but I immediately liked her partner, Dr. Klein, when she introduced herself and began to monitor my progress.

"We're going to have a baby within the hour!" she announced to me and my mom. I was very surprised by this prediction, just two and a half hours after my water broke.

My mom continued to keep Evan updated and check his location, and eventually he rushed through the door of my hospital room, laughing about the craziness of his morning travels.

My nervous excitement then turned to an almost surreal elation. *We're going to have a baby soon!*

Less than a half hour later, it was time to meet our new daughter.

# CHAPTER 3

## *"It's Her Skin"*

Evan had been convinced from the start of our pregnancy that the new baby would have two X chromosomes. Because I had guessed we would have a girl with my first pregnancy—only to be surprised when the sonogram tech drew a little baseball hat on our picture—I felt I really lacked mother's intuition in that department and wouldn't venture a guess the second time around. But I was simply so overjoyed to be pregnant again after nearly a year of trying that even the constant nausea through about the first eighteen weeks—and even sometimes after that—didn't deter me from wanting to savor every little thing about growing a child within me.

I knew, based on Evan's feelings on the subject, that this could be our last child, and I never took my hand off my growing belly, wanting to feel each flutter of movement and twinge of growth. It was not an especially easy pregnancy, between constant nausea and sciatic nerve pain in my last few weeks that left me hardly able to walk, but I never wavered in my gratitude to simply be pregnant.

Connor began to laugh at the way my belly button popped out, playfully pushing on it each time he noticed it. We moved him into his big boy room with a new red-and-navy-striped bedding set, and he started to call his old room "baby's room." I ate my way through each week, picking up steam as I felt better and better. And our list of names was forever changing, as we added and deleted and prioritized. Jaclyn, Leah, Charlotte. . .I kept discovering new names that I loved, but we wanted to meet our little girl before we gave her a name, just as we had with our Connor William.

At week twenty in my pregnancy, we had the typical sonogram, and everything was measuring as expected. Evan pressed the nurse, asking almost immediately if she could tell the sex, and she replied that she could. Did we want to know?

"Yes!" We held our breaths, and when we heard the word *girl*, there was an indescribable joy that radiated through my entire being. I wiped away tears as I thought about what that meant for our little family.

A boy and a girl. One of each, to experience everything with. A *daughter*. . .a daughter to dress in sweet little girl outfits, to shoot a basketball with, to teach how to apply makeup, to go prom dress shopping with, to watch walk down the aisle with her daddy on her wedding day. A daughter who would someday have children of her own, who would then come to me complaining about morning sickness and teething, just as I had with my mother.

"You are a perfect little girl!" I wrote after our twenty-week appointment in my pregnancy journal that filled up with photos and snippets of life as we prepared for our daughter. "Today was a wonderful day! During our ultrasound, we were able to see all four chambers of your heart and hear them all beating separately. We saw the blood flow from the umbilical cord into your body. You were holding your toes most of the time—it was so cute! Your profile looks a lot like your brother's!"

In our white hospital room on December 19, months after that appointment where we marveled at how "perfect" our baby looked and measured, I could hardly grasp how quickly delivery was happening, and my mind was flooding with our unexpectedly early arrival. *Will nursing be easier this time around? Will she be a good sleeper? (Please, yes.) Will she look like Connor? I'm so excited that we'll get to bring her to Christmas Day festivities and pass her around to adoring aunts and uncles. . . . Looks like we'll need to find a cute baby's first Christmas outfit!*

Before I could even think about resting, it was time to push. My parents left the room, and Evan assumed his position with the doctor and nurse, leaving our room quiet and focused. And after just twenty minutes, the head of our baby girl became visible.

I peered down to see Dr. Klein scrape, lightly, at the scalp a bit. And then she said words that will forever echo through my mind: "This is the thickest vernix I've ever seen."

Evan and I asked simultaneously, curious about this assessment, "What's vernix?"

"That cottage cheese-y stuff that is on babies when they're born," she replied.

I braced to push again, wishing there was a mirror on the ceiling like at Connor's birth, where I could see my baby emerge. As my last contraction eased and I temporarily stopped pushing, Dr. Klein continued to pull at the baby.

"She's just going to slide right out," she exclaimed, with a little surprise in her voice. And then our baby girl made her way out into a world that wasn't quite prepared for her and the uniqueness she brought with her.

The rush and excitement of childbirth immediately gave way to silence—shocked silence, as the whole room stopped and stared at the scene unfolding.

My vision felt a bit clouded, but I looked down at the whiteness that covered my daughter as Dr. Klein, out of habit, I'm sure, placed her on my chest. My baby lay on me with her head toward mine, but facing away from me, which meant that I hadn't yet gotten to see her precious face. But based on the abrupt silence in the room, I very gently, lightly placed my fingers on her head, wondering if I should even touch her.

*They just need to wipe her off,* I thought.

The thick vernix, I was sure, just needed to be wiped clean by the nurses.

But within seconds, the medical staff sprang to life. My baby girl was snatched from my chest as the nurses rushed to care for her. They began wiping her off on the infant warming bed, and I watched the circular rubbing over her body, feeling relieved and grateful that she would soon be free of the thick white gunk covering her tiny body.

With a pounding heart and eyes hazy from tears and emotion, the confusion and the panic in our big hospital room began to seep into me.

Evan had just enough time to snap a single photo of her birth, and after watching the nurse carefully but vigorously rubbing our baby down, he sank, lightheaded, into the green plastic couch with his face down while a nurse rushed to cover his head with a washcloth.

Another nurse—*How many are there now? They're seeming to multiply*—barked an order into the nearest intercom, requesting the presence of the neonatologist on duty immediately.

"She's in an operating room," the static answer came back.

"Get her in here *now!*" the doctor and nurses responded practically in unison, with an edge of panic in their voices.

A feeling of helplessness settled into me as I lay on the

hospital bed being attended to by Dr. Klein, still not able to feel most of my lower half from the anesthesia.

I wondered at first if my daughter could be stillborn, but then she began to cry loudly, protesting her exit from her warm and cozy home. *Surely her strong cry is a good sign?*

Dr. Klein had quickly cut the umbilical cord, and she began packing up the cord, cord blood, and anything else that might end up being beneficial to whatever was causing the medical staff to be panicked. She tried to smile at me, forcing her mouth up to reassure me, but her eyes were emotional with worry.

As Evan and I watched our newborn baby under the warming lamp, the realization came on slowly, and then all at once: the cleaning process was not effective at clearing the whiteness covering her body. The thick vernix that should have been wiped off with the nurse's towel wasn't vernix at all.

*It was her skin.*

# CHAPTER 4

## Redefining What We Know

The air was so cold that I sharply drew in a breath when I opened the car door. There wasn't a single person outside of the large building, but it was well lit and as inviting as possible. In fact, there was barely another car on the road.

But of course, at 11:00 p.m. on Christmas Eve, most families were at home—children sleeping fitfully, adults scrambling to create Christmas magic.

My dad had run every red light we encountered. I gingerly slid out of the passenger seat, still experiencing ligament tenderness and sciatic nerve pain from giving birth five days before.

Every step was heavy as the hospital doors automatically opened to a warm lobby, where the security guard handed me a visitor pass. I shuffled through the lobby, my husband's voice still playing out from his call from the neonatal intensive care unit, where he had been reading a bedtime story to our baby girl when test results came in.

"You need to get here now."

I glanced over to see a life-sized Nativity scene standing in the corner with an empty manger, waiting expectantly for a baby to be placed comfortably in the straw in just a few hours. And I began pleading with God: *Please don't let my daughter die on Christmas.*

Skin, our largest organ, is supposed to protect our bodies. Our skin keeps germs outside of our bodies, keeps water in our bodies so we stay hydrated, and helps to regulate our body temperatures, keeping us at a typical 98.6 degrees and sweating to cool ourselves off when heat threatens us.

Our daughter, Brenna Helen Marie, was born with skin that does not do these jobs well or at all.

Thanks to the quick actions of the neonatologist on duty, Dr. Darling, and our local pediatric dermatologist, Dr. Conlon, Brenna was cared for immediately after birth and transferred to the nearby neonatal intensive care unit, and we soon had a diagnosis: harlequin ichthyosis. Two words I had never heard of that took me days to be able to pronounce (har-la-kwin ick-thee-oh-sis, if you need help).

This condition is what is called autosomal recessive, which means that Evan and I had each unknowingly passed on a mutated gene to Brenna, causing an error in her genetic code. This mutation means her body does not produce a protein that helps her skin form correctly.

Because Brenna's body recognizes this error in its genetics, it tries to make up for it by producing skin much too quickly. This very rare disorder caused Brenna to be born with thick plaques of skin divided by deep, red fissures so raw that they looked bloody in many areas. Her skin was formed so tightly and so abundantly in utero that her ears could hardly be seen, and her eyelids were flipped inside out, revealing the inner red linings that were puffy and irritated. Her fingers and toes were shortened and clenched, imprisoned by hardened skin.

The first time I heard the words *skin condition* within an hour of giving birth to Brenna, the words hung in the air, not yet absorbing into my head. My internal reaction was that she would look a little different. . .and I began preparing myself with that realization. I believed it was simply an aesthetic issue. And I was very wrong.

The most critical health issues associated with harlequin ichthyosis at any stage of life are body temperature, regulation, dehydration because the skin doesn't hold water in well, and infection because the skin can't keep bacteria out. The deep fissures that covered Brenna's body at birth, cracking most severely in her joint areas, cause a high percentage of infants who are born with harlequin to die from excessive water loss or bacterial infections that penetrate the body through those cracks.

After she was admitted to the NICU, Brenna was kept in isolation and on morphine to help alleviate the pain caused by her skin, which was hard and cracking and raw. She mostly slept, sedated, in a closed isolette bed at a temperature of 98.6 degrees Fahrenheit, with such high humidity that it looked like a rain forest, to compensate for the fact that her skin couldn't hold its temperature or keep moisture in.

Every three hours, Brenna's nurse would open the little armhole doors of her covered plastic bed to gently feed her a bottle, coat her little body all over with an ointment called Aquaphor, and change her sleeping position.

Because the condition is so rare, there was not much research for us to read. Harlequin is just one of about twenty-eight different kinds of ichthyosis, all of which are genetic and range in severity. *Wikipedia* and other websites painted a very bleak picture of immediate prognosis for babies born with harlequin—words like *fatal* and *life threatening* jumped out at me with every click of the mouse.

I cringed when I read on *Wikipedia* about the first time that the condition was recorded in 1750. In the diary of Rev. Oliver Hart, a cleric from Charleston, South Carolina, was written:

> *On Thursday, April the 5th, 1750, I went to see a most deplorable object of a child, born the night before of one Mary Evans in "Chas"town. It was surprising to all who beheld it, and I scarcely know how to describe it. The skin was dry and hard and seemed to be cracked in many places, somewhat resembling the scales of a fish. The mouth was large and round and*

*open. It had no external nose, but two holes where the
nose should have been. The eyes appeared to be lumps
of coagulated blood, turned out, about the bigness of
a plum, ghastly to behold. It had no external ears,
but holes where the ears should be. The hands and
feet appeared to be swollen, were cramped up and felt
quite hard. The back part of the head was much open.
It made a strange kind of noise, very low, which I
cannot describe. It lived about forty-eight hours and
was alive when I saw it.*[1]

The shocking appearance was accurately described for the most part, but when it is your own child, it feels so harsh and wounding to see words like that.

I took information about this severe disorder slowly, relying on our medical team for answers and advice and mostly avoiding the Internet, at least for the first week or so. Just when I would begin to think that my mind had a grasp on what was happening and what kind of future might lie before us, more information would be added to send me into another tailspin of feeling overwhelmed, emotional, and, ultimately, grief stricken.

Throughout life, our sense of what is true in our world is constantly being challenged and changed in all kinds of ways—by what we read, by who we listen to, by the media

1. *Wikipedia*, s.v. "Harlequin-Type Ichthyosis," last modified 12/13/15, accessed 12/22/11, https://en.wikipedia.org/wiki/Harlequin-type_ichthyosis.

we absorb. But nothing affects us more than personal experience—the results of the choices we make and the events that directly affect our lives.

Our lives are often defined largely in our minds by our big moments: the wedding days, the state tournament championship, the college admittance letter or graduation, the first job offer. Of course, this includes the births of our babies. . .as well as deaths, diagnoses, job losses, tragic accidents.

Yet those big moments are led and followed by millions of tiny moments—the moments when we are reading, listening, learning, and feeling. Those tiny moments are what determine how we react to the big moments—how we celebrate, how we grieve, how we struggle, how we stand up again, and especially, how we *hope*.

Hope is a miraculous part of faith. Expectation and personal desire lie within hope, but there is mostly trust.

Even in the most dire and desperate of circumstances in this world, there is hope folded into the fear and the grief—hope for something better. And within each moment of our uncertainty and our anguish after Brenna was born critically ill and in pain, hope flowed in and out of our hearts, growing stronger as we placed all trust in God's hands.

A few days after Brenna was born, a family member said to me and Evan, "I haven't talked to God in years. . .but

I've actually been praying for Brenna." In that moment, I began to feel my worry transform into a faithful trust in God's purpose for her very significant life.

We met with the medical team in the NICU soon after Brenna's birth to discuss her prognosis and her future. It was then, as we spoke about pain management and minimizing infection risks instead of going home, that I fully started to comprehend how critical our baby girl's health was. Evan and I wiped tear after tear during that meeting as we emphasized to her doctors and nurses that our priority was to minimize the pain and discomfort that her hardened, cracked plaques of skin were causing—acknowledging that the likelihood of death was high, but regardless of the number of her days on earth, we as her parents wanted our precious daughter to endure as little pain as possible.

Five days after Brenna was born, we wrapped up our Christmas Eve celebration as traditionally as possible—family dinner eaten, Connor dressed in his snowman PJs, Christmas lights twinkling.

From the time I was a young child, the children's mass at our church has been my favorite—there is nothing more joyful and fulfilling on Christmas Eve than seeing it through the eyes of excited children—and so that night, I was determined for our family to attend our usual service, despite the stress of the last week.

During the entire mass, my mind would not leave my

baby girl, who was lying helplessly in her little incubator, struggling to breathe and experiencing pain each time she moved. Little girls—so many little girls that it made my heart ache—sat all around us with their families that evening, swishing their pretty velvety dresses back and forth, faces flushed with excited anticipation.

My friend Michelle, attending with her husband and three children, caught me at the end of mass, and as she gave me a tight hug, she whispered, "She'll be here next year." I wasn't sure I even believed that myself, but it was the most perfect thing she could say, and I nodded tearfully.

The entire evening was blurred with tears and anguish, burdened with our worries about Brenna, straining any attempts to enjoy our beloved Christmas Eve traditions. As the clock pushed on, Evan told me that he felt like he needed to go say good night to Brenna and read her a story, so he left for the hospital after we tucked Connor into bed.

Sitting at Brenna's quiet NICU bedside, Evan was reading the beautiful line from Nancy Tillman's *The Night You Were Born*, "Because there had never been anyone like you. . .ever in the world." Just then the alarm monitoring Brenna's lung saturation began to beep, and the numbers—which should be close to one hundred—dropped into the eighties.

The medical staff decided to draw a "blood gas," which is a test that monitors oxygen levels to see how well the baby is breathing. Their concern began to grow as Brenna showed no response to increased levels of oxygen supplied to her, and her blood gas results showed that her breathing was getting worse.

The neonatologist and nurse were sharing these results with Evan when another test result came in—blood work that was performed earlier that morning. Typically blood cultures take twenty-four hours to show results, but Brenna's came back positive for infection in thirteen hours, indicating a very aggressive bacteria trying to take over her body.

The ringing phone woke me up just an hour after I had fallen asleep, and it took me a moment to clear my head and realize what night it was.

"Brenna has an infection, and it's really serious," Evan told me softly, choking up. "You need to get here right now. It doesn't look good at all."

We summoned my parents so my mom could stay with sleeping Connor while my dad drove me to the hospital.

Our living room was dim, with only a side lamp offering light, and I unplugged the Christmas tree lights. Santa Claus had already made his stop at our house, and a modest pile of gifts was stacked around the six-foot tree. A bright red tricycle sat ready and waiting to be ridden by Connor, who had been excitedly pointing out bikes for the last two months.

My chest began to tighten, and I forced myself to slow my breaths, inhaling deeply and forcing out any anger that was rising in me. Saying good-bye was not supposed to happen on Christmas.

*Please, God, don't take my daughter on Your Son's birthday.*

When I heard a knock at the front door, I grabbed my bag and fell into my mom's arms, allowing tears to come then.

"It's too soon," I whispered.

# CHAPTER 5

## Holding On to Hope

The night guard at the hospital didn't even try to stop me for a visitor's badge, and my footsteps echoed through the lobby as I passed by the lovely lobby Nativity scene, still at least a half hour from its baby Jesus arriving.

I fell into Evan's arms in the doorway of Brenna's unit, and he breathed deeply, emotionally, as we held each other.

Evan and I were joined by my dad in Brenna's "pod," and we crowded around her incubator, watching her little chest rise and fall in short, rapid breaths. Her face was hard to make out, covered by a large hood providing oxygen to her, aiding her as she fought to stay alive.

Soon after arriving, Evan and I left Brenna's side to speak candidly with her doctor and nurse. They led us down the long central hallway of the unit and through a large room where at least eight tiny babies slept comfortably in open cribs. Little Santa hats sat on the ledges by some of the beds, and candy canes and homemade ornaments hung off the ends of others.

After a turn down another hallway, past the freezer that housed the small amounts of breast milk I had been pumping religiously for Brenna, we entered the family suite. Our shoulders slumped with the emotional drain, and our eyes were wet, red, and slightly swollen from crying for nearly five straight days.

If Brenna's breathing became worse, a decision would have to be made. We would need to decide whether to intubate her, which meant inserting a breathing tube down her throat into her lungs. This could be very difficult, particularly because of her skin, and would likely cause her a great deal of pain.

I felt my soul and my heart almost hovering outside of my body, which was numb with shock and grief. Did this mean what I thought it did? No, no, no. This was not happening to our beloved daughter. *Please, God, not on Christmas.*

So we asked the question—the one we had to say out loud as we grappled with the situation, the one that we already suspected the answer to. What would happen if we decided we didn't want our sweet baby girl to have to endure the kind of pain that attempting to intubate her would cause?

We clutched each other's arms, shaking with heartbroken sobs, when we were given an answer we never expected or thought we would ever hear: "We will make her as comfortable as possible while she passes."

Our minds thick with grief and disbelief, we decided that my mom needed to come to the hospital, and Evan made a very difficult call to his parents.

My in-laws had scheduled a trip to Europe to join Evan's sister, Alayna, after she had been studying abroad in Belgium for the last four months and to travel home with her. Two days before, we had urged Bill and Jeannine to go when they considered canceling because Brenna was stable at the time. Evan reached his parents, who were just waking up to a Belgian morning, and sobbed on the phone with his dad as he shared about Brenna's critical condition. His parents felt helpless and devastated thousands of miles away.

I remembered that my best friend, Kristin, was attending midnight mass with her family, so at 12:15 a.m. on Christmas Day, I reached her husband, Brian. My voice caught repeatedly as I tried to explain what was happening, and when Kristin took the phone, there was no hesitation as she assured me they would head straight to our house and Brian would drive my mom to the hospital.

When Mom arrived about a half hour later, Brenna's breathing was still rapid and labored but not worse. At that point, my mom brought up the subject of baptism, and we all agreed that we wanted Brenna to be baptized as soon as possible.

"I'm sorry it's so late, but Brenna is very sick," Evan's text message read. "Are you able to come baptize her as soon as possible?"

Evan's childhood pastor, Larry, always a calming and devoted presence who helped us to begin our family by uniting us in marriage, answered this desperate 1:00 a.m. plea and left his bed and his family to come dedicate Brenna to God.

It was, of course, not the baptism I had imagined when I planned for the birth of our little girl. I had pictured a sleeping baby dressed in the beautiful baptismal gown that I had worn as a baby. I had imagined us proudly holding her over the baptismal font, flanked by her godparents, with all of our family watching and praying.

It felt like the whole world was sleeping soundly, safely in their beds except for our tiny group crowded around our dying daughter—Evan and I, my parents, our two nurses, and our doctor. And when I sent a tearful text to Kristin, who is Brenna's godmother, to say, "WE ARE BAPTIZING BRENNA. I WISH YOU COULD BE HERE," her reply beeped several seconds later: "I'M THERE, MY FRIEND. I'M THERE."

Evan, Larry, and I washed our hands and pulled on medical gloves and yellow plastic hospital gowns. Our nurse, Kara, was thoughtful enough to offer to take photos, and I told her to take as many as she could.

With Brenna's incubator armholes opened, we lightly touched her side, which was heaving quickly up and down in short, labored breaths. Tears streamed down, blurring my vision and soaking my face, as Larry spoke poignantly about what a gift Brenna had been to our lives and to our family.

"Brenna Helen Marie, I baptize you in the name of the Father, and of the Son, and of the Holy Spirit," Larry proclaimed with grace and conviction, and my shoulders shook silently as I bit my lip to hold back a sob.

And truly, God's presence in our dark, quiet, crowded little hospital room was indescribably overwhelming.

I now know that when people describe a heavy heart, this is not figurative. That night, in the tear-filled quiet, my chest constricted under the weight of my aching heart, growing heavier with the indescribable pain of impending loss. . .but also with a kind of peace that Brenna's life had been given to God. Brenna's baptism felt like the one missing piece to her very short life that had now been completed, allowing me to feel at peace with saying good-bye, knowing she had been a cherished gift to us given by God and was ready to go home to Him whenever He willed it.

Following the baptism ceremony, we received news: Brenna's latest blood gas showed a very slight improvement in her breathing. And all we could do was wait—wait to see if Brenna's tiny body could fight to keep living, to keep breathing, to battle this aggressive infection.

As the clock neared 2:30 a.m., my mom and I decided that our bodies might be able to relinquish our emotions to sleep. We pulled out beds in the NICU's family suite where the doctor first delivered that evening's critical prognosis, and I made Evan promise me several times that he would come wake us the second anything changed in Brenna's condition.

For the next few hours, my mom and I dozed fitfully, and Evan and my dad perched in two high office-style chairs at Brenna's bedside to watch over her. The medical staff continually observed her and drew a blood gas every hour to monitor her breathing levels.

With each draw, there came a very slight improvement. It was so slight that it was not much to base any hope on, but that's the thing about hope: we always reach for it no matter the circumstances. Hope is what drives us in the darkness and pushes us to get back up when we have fallen.

With hope comes faith. And with faith, God reassures us in the book of Mark, nothing is impossible. "Sometimes," author Ann Voskamp once wrote, "we lay our hope, full and tender, into the depths of Him and wait in hope for God to resurrect something good."[2]

When Evan touched my arm at 5:30 a.m. to wake me from a fitful sleep, my chest immediately tightened, and I looked up at his face with alarm.

"Is she okay? What's going on?" I demanded.

He wearily delivered the news: "She is stable still; her

2. Ann Voskamp, "How to Keep Hoping When You Really Just Want to Give Up," *A Holy Experience* (blog), October 26, 2015, http://www.aholyexperience.com/2015/10/how-to-keep-hoping-when-you-really-just-want-to-give-up/.

tests are continuing to slightly improve."

Continuing improvement. . .and continuing hope.

My mom and I folded our beds back into couches and pulled on our shoes before returning to Brenna's bedside. Through her north-facing window, I could see the beginning streaks of the rising sun.

A new day. *Christmas Day.*

My shoulders sagged with the weight of what we all had endured over the last few hours—the pain and suffering of our daughter, pleading with God to let her live, having her baptized at 1:30 a.m. on Christmas Day as we cried over her helpless, hurting body. Though we were by no means certain that she would live, in the darkness of Brenna's little NICU pod we placed our faith in God, in hopes of what He might resurrect.

While my body and my heart had been with Brenna, my mind had also been flickering with thoughts of Connor and the traditional Christmas morning he was not going to get. Brenna's stability pushed us toward the respite of home. As the light grew brighter in Brenna's NICU pod, we decided to surrender the grief of the evening to the hope in the dawning of a new day.

As we walked slowly, wearily, toward the sliding glass doors that marked the entrance to the hospital, the bright winter sun streaming in seemed surreal.

I looked back at the lobby Nativity scene that I passed

just seven hours earlier, though it felt like twenty years.

And there was something new.

Baby Jesus lay gloriously in His manger, arms extended up to heaven, giving hope to all the world.

# CHAPTER 6

## *"Praise Him When We Win; Praise Him When We Lose"*

*I* would say we were blissfully unaware, but looking back, it was a superficial kind of bliss. It was a small comfort zone that we were dramatically and intentionally forced from. And we stepped out, blindsided, one toe at a time toward uneven terrain when all we thought we wanted was a smooth path.

But God met us, arms extended in that glorious Nativity scene, at the edge of the roughness and promised to walk us over each bump, each hole, each stretch of uncertainty or darkness.

Faith doesn't necessarily come from answered prayer or miracles or met expectations. No, what I have found is that faith comes from trust in God's will and God's greatness, regardless of what the world tells us we should believe. And sometimes we must fight every day to maintain that trust as the world pushes against it.

Knowing, truly knowing, that God is for us, not against us, gives us an endless hope and an unwavering trust no matter what happens in our lives.

The world of the neonatal intensive care unit is like

nothing I have ever experienced. When your newborn baby is taken immediately from her cozy home in your belly to a large plastic incubator, it feels like time stops.

You live in every day, every hour, and there is very little talk about the future because it is so uncertain and the second you start talking about the future, your baby's monitors loudly beep with alarm—a harsh reminder that anything can happen at any second to these fragile babies whose tiny bodies are fighting to live and to thrive.

And you live on faith alone—faith in God's plans, whatever they may be. You beg God for understanding and for healing. Hours spent in the NICU keeping watch over your baby sometimes feel like a standoff with God.

A few years ago, Evan and I watched the Christian film *Facing the Giants*, which is about a football coach who is facing several struggles, including losing his job and dealing with infertility as he and his wife try to have a baby. The one thing that stands out to me from that movie in the years since seeing it is something the coach tells his high school football players: "We praise God when we win, and we praise Him when we lose."

It is easy to say "thank You" to God when things are going right. It is a lot less easy to thank Him when we are faced with a devastating loss, a struggle, or any challenge, especially those that seem insurmountable.

We give God praise during the bright times—the

times when we are "winning." But we also need to praise Him during the dark times, when we feel like we're losing.

The days following Brenna's birth were some of my darkest times—days of confusion and sadness because I was so overwhelmed. I was living minute by minute, wondering if each day would be her last on earth.

During Brenna's first few weeks of life, I would get up at 2:00 a.m. for my obligatory breast milk pumping session once a night, and I chose to sit in the rocker in her room. Sometimes I was emotionally stable with being there, and I browsed Facebook or Pinterest, distracting my mind from the fact that I was determinedly pumping milk for a baby who might never be able to drink it.

But usually, I slowly rocked and cried while I pumped. I looked at each part of her room through my blurry tears, and I let my heart ache.

Her clothes, pretty little sleepers and dresses, all washed, hung expectantly in her closet. Would she ever get to wear them?

Her baby book lay on the floor, with a precious little hospital hat tucked into it, the one she never got to wear after she was born. Would I be able to fill in those pages with her likes and dislikes, her birthday party invitations and photos?

Her big pink frame hung above her dresser. Would there ever be a picture of a smiling family of four in it?

And her bed—her white wooden crib that we had so carefully picked out from the store just weeks before, with her bedding all washed and ready to comfort a sleeping child. I cried many nights as I stared at her bed, wondering if she would ever get to sleep there.

Instead of rocking my baby in this chair, I stored milk to take to the NICU each morning, carefully labeling and placing it in my container in the NICU freezer. We waited two long weeks before we were even able to hold our daughter in our arms, and otherwise, we could only interact with her every three hours.

At these three-hour increments, we got to touch our precious girl, and she heard our voices, though still probably muffled from the excess skin that filled her outer ear folds and canals. Our touch was bittersweet, however, as we pulled on yellow hospital gowns and medical gloves for each encounter. Our joy at handling our baby was tempered by trepidation, of whether we were clean enough or were hurting her with each movement.

And it broke my heart and angered me all at the same time to learn that many of the babies were there because of the lack of care they received while in utero: gestational diabetes that goes untreated, premature births with no prenatal care, drug-addicted babies who are slowly weaned off their addictions.

I did everything right. I went to all my appointments.

I drank that disgustingly sweet liquid at twenty weeks and got shots at twenty-eight weeks because of my negative blood type, which could have potentially attacked the baby if the baby's blood was positive. I counted kicks when I believed she wasn't moving enough, and I called my doctor to report it. I consumed minimal amounts of fish and caffeine and deli sandwiches (although, okay, maybe I ate too many Slim 4s from Jimmy John's because there were days when all I could stomach was a turkey sandwich). I slept on my right side to ensure proper blood flow. I read the big brother books with Connor, I decorated the nursery with splashes of bright pink, I washed her clothes in Dreft, and I talked to her every day. I told her I loved her every day, and I cried when I thought about how excited I was to be adding to our family. I prayed every night with Connor for "the baby to grow big and strong in Mommy's belly."

And it didn't matter.

We did everything we knew to do to deliver a strong and healthy child, and our daughter was still one of the sickest babies in the NICU. We did everything right, and we still faced so much uncertainty about being able to take our baby home.

God never promised fair, though. He did promise, however, to love us and to redeem us. He promised us the opportunity to spend eternal life with Jesus in heaven. And that promise alone is worthy of praising Him with our entire beings, every second of every day.

Gratitude allows us to see obstacles and hardships and disappointments in a new way, unfolding the raw and sometimes complex beauty of a situation that we previously never saw. As we strive to live the life that Jesus taught us, at the very center of that kind of living is praise—praise for our awesome God.

I often think about what it means to praise, to truly praise. Wrapped up in a life of praise is kindness and respect for God's creations, living with humility, and loving God and each other with all our hearts.

But at the center of praise is gratitude.

Within everything we do to praise and to exalt and to rejoice and to worship. . .we *thank*.

Gratitude moves within us slowly and quickly, consciously and subconsciously. Sometimes we are completely overwhelmed by gratitude at a moment of sheer beauty—everything from receiving good news about a major life event to that tiny piece of time when your toddler's giggles erupt so fiercely that your heart and your mind are nowhere but that brilliant moment of joy.

But at other times we must constantly seek out gratitude. It becomes a choice, again and again. And yet, as we fight to choose thanksgiving, that decision, hour after hour, builds upon itself to create a whole day of feeling more grateful than not. And then two days. And then a week. And suddenly, even in the darkest of times, we find that we have discovered a life of gratitude, of *praise*. With that kind of gratitude and praise comes true joy, peaceful contentment.

Sometimes, when words escape me, I simply pray, "Thank You." *Thank You, Lord, for this life, for what You are doing in my life, and for the greatest gifts of Your love and of Your sacrifice.*

Whatever happens today, whatever happens tomorrow, and whatever happened yesterday, we can still praise.

We can praise God even when we don't understand or agree. We can praise Him in the good times when it is easy to thank Him and feel His presence and His glory. But more importantly, we can—and should—praise Him in the bad times. . .times when we wonder how He could "let" something happen or if He's even there with us at all. Because He is there; we might just have to look a little harder to see Him, but He is always there.

Praise Him when we win; praise Him when we lose— looking for beauty and for gratitude in every day, in every experience.

# CHAPTER 7

## What a Difference a Day Makes

The skies were deep gray and wet, not holding any promises of much more color as the day progressed. My plane taxied on the runway, and I breathed deeply, always a little nervous about flying and the absurdity of this large metal machine being able to coast through the air.

The plane shifted and lifted, the bottom jolting and bumping as the wheels retracted and we rose upward.

The dark and drizzly surroundings suddenly turned foggy as we hit the clouds, and I strained to see the words of the book I held in my lap. I considered how terrifying it would be to fly a plane when you couldn't see what was directly in front of you.

But then, suddenly, my pages were illuminated, and I turned to look out the tiny window. White puffs were just below the wings, and the plane had burst into the sunlight that was no longer obstructed by the clouds.

What a difference those two points are.

In the clouds, you can allow the low visibility to overtake your emotions and sense. There may be anxiety, fear, even panic. You may even want to pull back down to the ground, feeling the urge to retreat back to what you know, what feels certain and familiar.

Yet, a couple of seconds later, a couple of inches higher, there is brilliance. There is the beauty and glory of the sun— and with that, there is relief, confidence, hope, affirmation to keep going, to keep rising.

Two points of life, right next to each other. Do you have the trust and drive to keep rising?

The day Brenna was born, I began learning how God meets us in that dark gray. He carries us through the foggy clouds when we cannot see. We may not be able to view for ourselves which direction we need to go, but we can trust God to lead us.

And He lifts us into the light, past the dark, past the clouds and the obstacles that render us unable to see but still able to trust.

How will we ever know what God holds for us within each story we are living, that the most glorious goodness of life is within reach, is about to meet us if we stop striving. . .trying. . .rising? Without completely trusting in His strength, His guidance, and His sovereignty, that light is out of reach.

There is a photo of me in front of our little Christmas tree days before Brenna's birth. Christmas decorations were sparse that year as we anticipated the arrival of our little girl soon after the holidays, not wanting the extra responsibility having to put away ornaments and Nativity scenes. In the photo, I'm standing sideways, belly bulging in a gray-and-black-striped maternity shirt that I wore practically every day that fall.

Today, I hardly recognize that young woman in the photo.

The mother standing in this picture had visions of so many things dancing in her head about having a daughter. . .so many things that weren't important. The mother in that photo was picturing cute little swimsuits, pink twirly dresses, crushes on her brother's friends, teenage fights about too-tight clothing. Would she be smart, would she be athletic, would she be popular?

I became a different person on December 19, 2011. It didn't happen all at once, but that was the day that God firmly took hold of my heart and began to slowly mold and change me. That was the day that God gave me a choice about whether to embrace the gifts in this world, to embrace the perfect and unique differences that He placed into my life—or whether to run toward resentment and bitterness.

And it was not simply a matter of accepting my daughter as she was born and as God created her. No, He moved much deeper than a mother's unconditional love for her child. I felt Him challenge me, day after day, to tear down the preconceptions and the misconceptions of life as I knew it.

Up to that day, life had been relatively easy. Life isn't as complicated when you think you know everything, think you have the answers, and quickly fit everything and everyone into labeled black-and-white boxes.

In this life, it takes a lot of guts to stand up and say, "I know the answer." I was always timid about raising my hand in class, for fear of being wrong, even when I knew the answer. But what I'm realizing is that it actually takes a whole lot more courage to stand up and say, "I don't know the answer. But I'm willing to listen and learn and love, even if there is not one clear answer."

Within our lives, there comes a day when we determine the way we want to live—the values we prioritize, the ideals our hearts encompass, the attitudes we adopt—as taught to us by Jesus our Savior. We need to embrace the day we choose to be different, to live differently, and begin to make consistent decisions to stand for that difference that Jesus modeled for us, even when the rest of the world is running in the opposite direction.

And the world will be a whole lot richer on the day we all agree that even living in accordance with God's ideals and beliefs can look different, as we all make decisions for our family about what schools our children will attend, what food they will eat, what kind of discipline to use, and so much more.

Micah 7:7 declares, "But as for me, I watch in hope for the LORD, I wait for God my Savior; my God will hear me."

As for me, I will look to God; I will rely on the Lord.

Living within God's unique purpose and calling day after day is rarely easy or comfortable—not when we have a whole other world telling us the way we should be living and what we should be valuing and what we should look like.

But when we decide what we value and what is important to us, we can build a life of positive action around that.

In her book *Kisses from Katie*, Katie Davis describes her life-altering decision to rely on God's calling for her life as she moved to Uganda to minister to the sick and poor and adopted thirteen daughters as her own. When people questioned this decision to exchange her comfortable life in Tennessee for the uncertainty and poverty of Uganda, Katie simply knew God was using her for His purpose, to love His children.

She writes in her book, "God has a way of using inadequate people, and sometimes He calls us to reach a little higher or stretch a little further, even when we feel we can't do any more. We simply trust Him. And then, He gives us everything we need to do the 'more' that He is asking of us."[3]

I think there are two ways we can approach the hardships, the obstacles in our lives.

3. Katie Davis, *Kisses from Katie* (Brentwood, TN: Howard Books, 2012), 109.

We can lament, "God, how could You?" We can put blame and anger on our loving Father. *How could You let this happen?*

Or we can call out to Him: "God, I need You."

We can reach for Him in the darkness. *I need You, Lord—Your love, Your guidance, Your sovereignty. Your promise of hope.*

One day as my sorority sister Kate pushed her son on the swing, she was feeling a bit off. . .in a place where she couldn't shake an uneasy feeling of lacking control. Three underdogs in, her son looked up at the sky as he swayed and said, "Mommy, when I do this, it feels like I'm falling!"

She recognized immediately this feeling of lack of control in her own life, feeling that same feeling of "falling," but then she heard herself respond, "Are you falling, buddy. . .or are you flying?"

What is the difference? Where exactly is that point of difference between flying and falling?

"It's a choice of intention," Kate writes on her blog, HelloKateJ.com. "Will you embrace the freedom of the air or panic at what might be to come? Will you spread your wings with trust and faith or will you flap like crazy with terror in your heart? Will you soak up the view or close your eyes tight?"[4]

---

4. Kate Johnson, "Falling or Flying," hellokatej.com (blog), October 7, 2015, http://www.hellokatej.com/blog/falling-or-flying.

"After all," Kate notes, "sometimes recognizing fear isn't in itself enough to make it go away. There are times we have to embrace it, learn from it and use it to inspire us toward something more."

Sometimes it takes powerful intention to stand up against the grain. Sometimes it takes powerful intention to live "as for me." And sometimes it takes powerful intention to keep rising when we feel afraid, simply praying for light and a safe landing.

There are dark, cloudy circumstances in each of our lives—moments when we feel out of control, moments when we don't know the answer, moments when we feel as though we are falling. But there is the promise of light, too, and often there is a choice between the differences of those two points.

That difference relies on how much trust we place in God for guiding our lives and our hearts, leading us from the darkness into the brightness.

When Brenna was born, God offered me Himself and His love and guidance. He offered me the gift of redefining what beautiful was and what it meant in my life. And I felt this question rolling through my mind: Could I boldly lean into this new life, at the risk of enduring struggle and hardship, reaching for what God might show me in the way of *His* beautiful—a different beautiful than I had ever known or conceived before?

Often, the gray is rocky. There is turbulence and darkness and obstacles. But resistance creates lift. For those who keep holding on, who keep rising, and who open their eyes and their arms, there is brilliant light.

# CHAPTER 8

## Pigtails

$\mathcal{E}$van always told me he didn't do girl hair.
Ponytails, pigtails, braids—forget it.

Evan grew up with two sisters and has laughed over the years that any attempts to brush a ponytail up turned disastrous. And since then, his stylist skills have been little used.

As our second pregnancy progressed and we envisioned our little girl, we saw pigtails—blond, wispy pigtails pulled up on the sides of our daughter's head, bouncing as she toddled curiously and playfully around our home.

On the night Brenna was born, Evan met some of our doctors at the NICU and had a very difficult and emotional conversation about her prognosis. The neonatologists simply didn't know if they would be able to keep her alive. We were fortunate that she was admitted to a wonderful pediatric hospital called St. John's Children's Hospital with an immensely capable medical team, but the doctors had never seen her condition before, and she was in an extremely critical state.

Brenna lay in her little isolette, barely moving as her thick skin encapsulated her body, every part of her looking raw and painful. All the shock and emotions of her birth eventually released, and Evan sobbed as our vision of bouncy blond pigtails was ripped from his mind.

Growing hair was something we gave up on early in Brenna's life. Of course, hair was not, and never has been, important to us, and we accepted very early on that she could possibly be mostly bald for her entire life, unless she decides to wear a wig—a choice we are leaving completely up to her.

Brenna's skin disorder, harlequin ichthyosis, typically causes hair growth to be very sparse because the body makes so much skin that it kills off hair follicles. The hairline is usually receded, with hair in patches around the head, depending on how the skin is shedding. Brenna has a few eyelashes that come and go, and when she was around two and a half, we noticed a light smattering of eyebrow hair above her bright blue eyes.

When Brenna was born, we could see clumps of dark hair grown into her thick plates of skin. As those original plaques of skin began to peel off, they took her hair with them.

As parents, I think sometimes we put too much stock in things like hair—things that we dream about but aren't really important.

I not only envisioned a little girl in pigtails when I rubbed my round pregnant belly, but I imagined lathering up the heads of both of my wiggling kids in the bathtub together and showing my daughter how to curl her hair with a hot iron or pinning back an updo for prom.

But in that little hospital pod, just a week after she was born, I traded in those expectations. And I felt absolutely no loss because peeling back the patches of armor-like skin was so liberating that I didn't give a second thought to the hair that was peeled off with it. The plaques of skin on her head were the last to go, and it was as if Brenna was a butterfly emerging from her chrysalis. Losing her hair with her skin meant she was more comfortable and at less risk for infection, so it was easy for me to let go of, at least in those moments.

In the first year of Brenna's life, there wasn't much hair to contend with, but as she grew older, tufts of white-blond hair began to emerge from her scalp around the back of her head. And that same dad who was adamant that he didn't do girl hair? Well, he became the primary caretaker of Brenna's emerging locks.

It all started because of bath-time positioning.

Brenna's skin requires a long bath each day, and it always will. In the bath, her body soaks up the moisture, and her extra skin is softened in the water. Each day, her skin builds up, and each day in the bath, we scrub off those softened skin layers.

In our first home, the bathtub was tucked into the corner with the toilet next to it. Because I am much smaller than my six-foot-four husband, I ended up with "bottom half" duty, as I wedged next to the toilet, balanced on the side of the tub, in order to scrub the excess skin from Brenna's feet, legs, and torso.

Evan faced me on the other half of the tub, exfoliating Brenna's head, back, neck, and arms.

At first, her head was easy, simply an extension of the skin on her back and neck. After the original plaques of hardened skin finally fell off and took all hair with them, the skin on her head was smooth and bald.

But over time, despite the constant scrubbing, tiny, persistent hairs grew in.

And now, every day during Brenna's long bath, Evan spends the majority of his time on Brenna's scalp, first rubbing over and over in circular motions with a washcloth in a way that is both gentle and vigorous.

Then, he so carefully and so lovingly combs out her hair, gently picking the comb from the very bottom of her scalp so that by the time he is done, the comb contains clumps of skin, Brenna's scalp is smooth, and her hair is beautifully full and brushed out.

Evan not only "does" girl hair, but he is the sole reason Brenna has as much hair as she does.

For him, I think it's a tangible way to express love for his daughter. He is most focused on getting the excess skin off her scalp, so that her head is less itchy and less at risk of an infection, which could happen if her skin layers are allowed to build up and crack open. Evan jokes that if it were up to him, he'd buzz her hair, to make his job of removing skin easier. But he says Brenna's hair has become important to him because he thinks it will be important to her when she is older.

Evan preserves his daughter's hair with fierce protection and love, just in case we have a ten- or fifteen-year-old girl who wants little braids or to brush her own hair instead of a wig.

One evening when Brenna was two years old, I prepared as usual for her postbath routine while Evan completed his scalp care. I laid out her Minnie Mouse pajamas, grabbed her towel from the linen closet, and got out her ear curette, a tiny tool with a little hook on the end that we use to scoop out the excess skin in her ear folds and ear canals that build up every day.

Evan was taking longer than usual to finish up bath time, and just as I was about to ask if he was almost done, he laughed loudly and called out to me from the bathroom.

"Look at this!"

I peered over his shoulder into the tub as I entered the bathroom.

Evan was smiling as he gently twisted and retwisted the tiny curly hairs near the base of Brenna's neck.

And there they were.

*Our blond pigtails.*

We laughed, we took pictures, and we exclaimed to Brenna how beautiful her hair looked as she proudly patted her head.

Suddenly, fashioning our daughter's hair into pigtails became so much more special than we could have ever imagined.

And since that precious moment, I've come to realize how often the rest of life is like that. Sometimes, when something is different than we anticipated or hoped for, it leaves us disappointed, confused, or grieving a kind of loss.

Hurdles often come up in life, or we face the unexpected on our way to living out our dreams. We expect one thing and end up with another, and that feels like failure or letdown or disappointment or loss.

Too often we see things for what they aren't—how something *doesn't* look, how something *didn't* happen.

We agonize over the phone call that didn't come, the one with that job offer we dreamed about. We dwell on the one missed basket at the crucial point in the game. We beat ourselves up for using formula when we had planned to breast-feed our newborn. We are disappointed when our child chooses a different college than the school we had hoped he would attend.

We all go through seasons of life where we experience something different than what we were expecting.

But so much of life is like Brenna's pigtails.

When Evan and I first thought about our daughter's pigtails, the thought certainly didn't cross our minds that she might not be able to grow much hair, or that we may only ever be able to twist fine curls of hair into tiny pigtails at her neck.

And there were times when we mourned the loss of her hair, along with the loss of many other things we expected about adding a little girl to our family.

That evening, when two tiny twists of hair emerged on her head to form pigtails, they weren't the kind of pigtails we imagined. But they were so much more beautiful. To me, Brenna's barely there pigtails stand for years of hard work, love, and care. . .especially care from her daddy. To witness a father's tender acts of hair care, and the joy that comes from playfully styling that hair into little Mohawks and twisty pigtails, brings so much beauty into our lives.

That beauty comes in the form of admiration for my husband, building a marriage that is stronger despite the demands of caring for a child with severe health needs.

That beauty comes in the form of family bonding and cultivating relationships filled with love as we all gather around the bathtub to laugh and talk.

And that beauty comes in the form of appreciation for all that we have, especially each other, which creates contentment in our hearts.

Our family strives each day to celebrate that kind of beauty for what it is and what it looks like, instead of dwelling on what it isn't.

Sometimes we may need to step back to see things for the beautiful that they are and could be. Sometimes beauty in our lives looks so different than what we expected that we can't even see it at first.

But I think most of the time, what we first grieve as a loss or disappointment in our lives eventually reveals itself as a beautiful experience if we open our eyes to recognizing how God is present and is sharing Himself in all kinds of ways and through all kinds of people.

We all have our own expectations and dreams of pigtails, and some, maybe even most, of those may not end up looking like we had planned. But when we can see the beautiful in the unexpected, we learn to find joy and celebration in what is, instead of mourning what isn't.

# CHAPTER 9

## Chasing Normal

*I* grew up on a quiet cul-de-sac composed of fifteen homes newly built in the 1980s, on a growing side of town with younger families in just about every house. My two best friends lived in the same subdivision, and back when children roamed more freely, we used to walk back and forth to each other's houses all summer long and meet at a specific corner to ride our bikes to school together.

A family who lived across the street had two girls several years older than me. One of them, Elizabeth, was one of my favorite babysitters. And Elizabeth's older sister, Leanne, has Down syndrome.

I don't remember any kind of epiphany of recognizing this but just a general understanding that Leanne was a little different, and I was a bit timid as a young girl because I couldn't always understand exactly what she was saying. She spoke quickly and enthusiastically but not always clearly enough for me to grasp her words. This never made me avoid her, but for whatever reason, it embarrassed my shy self a bit.

As we all grew older, I remember the amusement that came from the sweet stories Leanne would bring home from school and her bus ride—stories that usually involved a boy she had a crush on.

Elizabeth ended up moving away, getting married, and starting a family. And when it came time for her and her husband, Travis, to decide to become parents, they first chose the route of adoption. Their little blond-haired, blue-eyed baby Josie also has Down syndrome—a very instinctive choice inspired by Elizabeth's loving relationship with her sister.

"There was never a day in my life that I lived outside of the Down syndrome community. Down syndrome was as natural to me as breathing," Elizabeth writes on her blog, *Confessions of the Chromosomally Enhanced.*[5]

"There was never any process where I had to learn to accept Leanne and her diagnosis; she was a part of my family since the day I entered the world and as younger siblings tend to do, I thought my older sibling was the coolest person ever."

Elizabeth admits that, in looking back on her children, she now sees how she was perhaps blissfully naive in her thinking, because she always held such a positive view of the special-needs community. And it wasn't until she re-entered this community as a parent that she realized how many people did not share her overwhelmingly positive

---

5. Elizabeth N., "Defining Perfection," *Confessions of the Chromosomally Enhanced* (blog), June 9, 2015, http://www.confessionsofthechromosomallyenhanced .com/2015/06/defining-perfection.html.

opinion of individuals with disabilities. She watched parent after parent in the Down syndrome community express sadness, fear, and mourning for their child's diagnosis.

"It was hurtful to experience the negative attitudes that exist out there. So many people still see individuals like my sister and daughter as flawed; like they somehow fall short of what constitutes an ideal human being," she says.

When it comes to what the ideal hair color, skin type, eye color, height, and weight are, the answers to these questions, Elizabeth notes, are both subjective and insignificant. "And if you spend your time dwelling on these qualities, you're missing out on the truly important qualities that people have to offer," she says.

Now the parents of two more sweet girls, Merryn and Lydia, Elizabeth and Travis are grateful they are able to give all of their daughters the opportunity to experience a piece of the world that defaults to accepting and positive, as she has experienced in the special-needs community.

Despite extra challenges they have faced with the developmental delays that often accompany Down syndrome and with Josie's health in general, including a very critical period when Josie was a baby, Elizabeth's family has carved out a "normal" for their family where differences play an extraordinary and positive role in life.

After Brenna joined our family, normal became something I wished for, hoped for, cried over.

And then it happened, without me even realizing it.

It was a relaxing winter afternoon as I sat with Brenna and Connor in our living room, playing with toys and pulling out books to read, and it dawned on me: our lives finally felt "normal." Of course, they weren't. At least, not what the majority of the world would consider normal.

But I'm not sure anyone lives a truly normal life because normal is only a concept based on our tiny little pocket of the world and what we know within our own experiences. What's normal in the United States is not normal in Africa, and what's normal for one generation of people is not for the next. Normal is entirely based on perception.

And a year after Brenna was born, this severe skin condition that rocked our world and everything we had previously known and believed had finally become normal to me.

It felt normal to slip on medical gloves to cover my baby's body in thick Aquaphor ointment every day, several times a day. It felt normal to measure out bleach to add to her bath to kill any unwanted bacteria. It felt normal to hook up tubing to pump in formula through a gastronomy tube in Brenna's stomach. And it felt normal to try to gently massage Brenna's tiny fisted fingers open when we played. In my mind, this was all no longer unusual; this had become my normal as a mother to my two children.

In her book *Rare Bird*, Anna Whiston-Donaldson

notes, "It's easy to be caught up in the standards of the world when your kid operates beautifully within the structure of what is normal."[6]

When Connor was young, I would look forward to the checkups with his physician. I couldn't wait to see how much he'd grown, and I would proudly mark off just about every question on the doctor's evaluation with "always." Yes, he *can* pull up. Yes, he *can* say two-word sentences. Yes, he *can* color a straight line.

I developed a misplaced pride in not only what he could do but what that must mean for me as a parent, too. However, when I began to take Brenna in for her regular checkups, that pride was tossed right back in my face.

Those check marks? They rarely find their way into the "always" category now. For the first year of Brenna's life, I'd feel like throwing the evaluation back in the nurse's face and saying, "She can't do any of these things, so *what's your point?*"

Today, I still mark "yes" and "always" for most of Connor's developmental evaluations, and I do mark "never" or "sometimes" on most of Brenna's. But now, I don't give it a second thought beyond that simple check mark.

Because I see every day how much they both are *learning* and *progressing* and *trying* in all different areas—areas that are important but that the doctor's offices don't measure. Areas like kindness and empathy and creativity

6. Anna Whiston-Donaldson, *Rare Bird* (New York: Convergent Books, 2015), 108–9.

and imagination and respect and building relationships and friendships.

I used to think those evaluations actually meant something more, perhaps even helping to measure what a dedicated mother I was. My child was operating very successfully within this arbitrary structure of normal, and I placed so much value in what that said about my parenting.

Our cousin Caitlin and her husband, Jeff, have a sign hanging in their bathroom that says, DON'T BELIEVE EVERYTHING YOU THINK.

Sometimes we go about our lives without ever questioning why we do what we do and why we think what we think. We believe what we've been told without question. We do what we've always done, without question.

We simply buy into whatever we come across or read or are told without stepping back to consider whether it makes sense to us within our own lives. And whatever we do and say and think then carries the label of "normal"— and anything that falls outside of our little pocket of life is "not normal."

But labeling the way people look and their abilities as normal and not normal is such a dangerous game to play. Trying to operate our lives under the structures of what we believe is normal (and not) leads to minds and hearts that are closed off from wanting to understand, to empathize, to feel and express compassion. Living this way means we can never learn to accept and celebrate anything that is outside of our realm of normal. We can never fully appreciate the amazing uniqueness God has placed in this world.

Mainstream society has a way, especially within advertising, of pushing us into a certain course of action or way of thinking—simply because "that's the way it is." Sometimes we forget to ask ourselves, *Is there a good reason for this? Is it really necessary? Is this what I truly believe? Or am I just doing this or thinking this because it's what my parents did, what my friends told me, or what I've always done?*

In recent decades—especially in this millennium—we seem to be starting to realize that looking like the covers of popular magazines is actually not the norm. We are actually all incredible creations who are formed in a multitude of sizes, shapes, colors, and even abilities.

*Because of this, normal truly doesn't exist.*

It is up to each one of us to take a stand against trying to fit our extraordinary lives into this meaningless label and instead to begin to share—with each other and especially with our children—this idea of all different kinds of normal. . .all different kinds of beautiful.

In a blog post called "You Are What You Share," marketing and communications guru Seth Godin writes: "We live in an ever-changing culture, and that culture is changed precisely by the ideas we engage with and the ones we choose to share. Sharing an idea you care about is a generous way to change your world for the better.

"It takes guts to say 'I read this and you should too.' The guts to care enough about our culture (and your friends) to move it forward and to stand for something."[7]

If we try to chase "normal," we will be left running in circles. The best kind of normal for our lives is to allow differences to play an exciting and positive role in shaping us. Ultimately, our ability to conform does nothing for the world. Instead, Godin writes, "We'll judge you most on whether you care enough to change things."

7. Seth Godin, "You Are What You Share," sethgodin.typepad.com (blog), January 16, 2015, http://sethgodin.typepad.com/seths_blog/2015/01/you-are-what-you-share.html.

# CHAPTER 10

## Blinders

*I*t is common practice to put an object around the eyes of horses. For racehorses or driving horses, these objects, called blinders, block the view on the sides of the horses' eyes so the horses cannot see behind or beside them.

The purpose of blinders is to help the horse focus. Blinders eliminate distractions so that the horse can focus on what is in front of him.

In 2014, our family attended our first National Family Conference that was hosted by the Foundation for Ichthyosis and Related Skin Types (also known as FIRST). FIRST is the only advocacy and research organization in the United States for people with Brenna's skin condition, ichthyosis. With a wide range in the severity of the disorder, some of these children and adults look very similar to Brenna, while others have darker patches, more hair, or only certain areas of skin affected, such as their hands and feet.

Before the conference, messages about the conference were flying around on social media from the excited families affected by ichthyosis who would be attending from all over the world.

One of the comments particularly struck me from a mom whose family had attended the conference before in past years. She wrote that it is interesting to see the new types of stares from the children at the conference—not the kind of stares that convey "What's wrong with that kid?" but instead, "Oh my goodness, that child's skin looks like *mine!*"

On the morning of our first breakfast at the conference, I started to tell Evan about this mother's observation. "It's a new experience for the kids to see other kids who look like them," I explained.

We sat in a banquet room surrounded by children and adults alike with various forms of this rare skin disorder. A simple glance around the room revealed skin of all kinds—from red and flaky to thick and dry, peeling, and coated in Aquaphor for moisture.

And before Evan could respond, Connor interjected, "Why do they look the same?"

Not wanting to attempt to explain the entire story, I told him not to worry about it.

But in usual four-year-old fashion, he pressed on. "Is it their *hair?*"

Evan and I locked eyes over Connor's head, silently asking each other the same question: How did he not see the differences in everyone's skin?

Maybe in doing so, I avoided the question, but I

decided not to point out the physical differences between many of the people there to Connor because he didn't see them. And we wanted to keep those blinders on his little four-year-old eyes for as long as possible.

We spent three days in Indianapolis with hundreds of other people of all kinds of sizes, ages, and skin types, and not once did Connor ask about anyone's appearance.

Perhaps God puts blinders on us that society eventually removes. As babies born into this world, we seem to be blind to visual differences. And then the culture of our modern world steps into our lives.

We don't view body parts as too big or too small until we are taught to judge as such by others. We delight in the color in our world until our culture paints a different picture for us that colors can be good and bad—often injecting that picture with hate or fear. We see personalities and love as "pretty" until we learn what advertising teaches us is "pretty."

Slowly, over time, the blinders given to us by God come off, and we lose focus. And often, as the world removes our blinders, it also peels off our own confidence and self-assurance and our respect and acceptance of others.

Blinders are metaphorically used today to describe someone with a narrow focus.

God shared with us the importance of having a narrow focus when it comes to truly seeing people. First Samuel

16:7 tells us, "'The LORD does not look at the things people look at. People look at the outward appearance, but the LORD looks at the heart.'"

The Lord has a narrow focus. . .one focus. Our hearts.

And it is too easy for people today to lose the blinders that keep us focused on the heart.

We are distracted.

As we buy into the beauty standards that our culture has set, we become so very distracted by difference, and we lose focus on the heart and on the heart's utmost importance to defining our beauty.

Somehow, God's blinders still very much remain on my son, even as a six-year-old. Connor doesn't see appearances; he sees people. He notices what people are doing and what they are saying before noticing what they look like.

For years, Connor had absolutely no idea that Brenna's skin is different. He attributed much of her health care needs to the simple fact that she was a baby—even very specialized needs like having a gastronomy tube in her tummy and being completely tube-fed for a year and a half.

I occasionally wondered when and how both of my kids would realize Brenna's physical differences. And I knew they would have different levels of understanding as they both grew older.

And then one day, as we drove along on a back country road on our way to a friend's house, it finally came.

Connor piped up from a quiet backseat as we listened to country music on the radio. "Remember when that person didn't know that Brenna has special skin?"

I didn't expect it. And so I stalled, trying to decide how to respond. "Which person?" I asked him.

"I don't know." He shrugged.

"Yes," I said carefully. "Sometimes we just need to tell people when they don't know, don't we?"

"Yeah."

And then, from the other side of the car: "Special skin!"

Brenna exclaimed the words, and with her left hand, she pointed to her right arm and rubbed her finger along the crook of her elbow.

"Special skin," she repeated.

I felt like I'd been found out, like I had a huge secret and my kids had guessed what it was. And quite honestly, I felt a twinge of sorrow—much more so for them than for me.

So many people had asked about Brenna's skin that my children overheard me explain "special skin" enough to make it part of their everyday vocabulary. And this hurts because Brenna's skin is what these people notice—not only first but more than anything else about her. Of course people may notice her skin first, because it stands out. But many times, that is all they see, without taking the time to focus on anything else—including our feelings.

And truth be told, I wish I could protect my kids from this forever.

Because right now, it is simply "special skin." But I know it will eventually morph into them noticing kids (and adults) staring or hearing harsher language, like "What's wrong with your sister?" Or worse. And the responsibility of having to teach my children how to respond to each new question, comment, or point is daunting.

As my kids grow, right now I simply strive to teach them how to keep their blinders on so they can stay focused on the hearts of others. Through this vantage point, I hope that they may, in turn, show the people around them how to stay focused on what is important in a way that is graceful, kind, and self-assured, regardless of what comes their way.

In our house, we try to keep the emphasis off looks. When we read books, we don't point out the character's outfit that looks silly because we don't want our kids to learn to judge others by what they choose to wear. We don't describe pink as a "girl color" or blue as a "boy color" because colors are simply colors, and all kinds of different people like all kinds of different colors. And exercising is to feel better and healthier, not to look better.

The more my kids are becoming aware of the world, the more I'm realizing how much emphasis is placed on appearance and looks and difference in a negative way. We often instill these sayings and values into our kids without even thinking about it. I have to catch myself not to only affirm my kids as beautiful and handsome when they are all dressed up but when they do something kind, generous, or helpful.

A swirly skirt doesn't make us more beautiful, but we are so conditioned to compliment people when it comes to how they look. "You look so great in that dress!" is unfortunately much more common than conversations that start with, "What a wonderful job you did volunteering for that fund-raiser. You are so caring and compassionate!"

I realize that the removal of our blinders by culture is seemingly inevitable as we learn about the world. As children, we are taught day in and day out how to distinguish things, how to tell items apart, how to choose "the one that is not like the rest."

As parents, we need to push back a little, to keep the focus where it should be. When it comes to telling things apart, our children need to be taught how to tell right from wrong, how to tell kind from unkind, how to tell what's respectful from rude, and how to tell compassion from apathy.

Even in biblical times, people looked at "outward appearance." Outward appearance has, from the beginning of time, served as a basis of judgment from others.

But the Lord looks at the heart. And we have the

opportunity, every day, to glorify God by looking at the heart, too.

I recently read a quote by John Steinbeck, author of *The Grapes of Wrath* and *Of Mice and Men*, that said, "I wonder how many people I've looked at all my life and never seen."

In putting our blinders back up, we can narrow our focus. And we can choose to teach our children how to not be distracted by the unimportant and how to focus on the heart.

The fashion magazines will always be there, with their own standards of what is cover material.

But it is our own personal decision to not be distracted by this. This decision is made each and every day. Every time we meet someone new, every time we decide which words to use in a situation, every time we look in the mirror, we are given the opportunity to put our blinders on, to focus on the heart.

Seeing the "big picture" is a catchphrase often used in society today, even described as an essential quality for leadership. And viewing the whole instead of the parts, especially for the future of an idea or a business, usually results in the ability to move that idea or business forward and upward.

But when it comes to people, there is just one part that is more important than others. And that part is not visible to the eye. In looking at others, we need to take a cue from our leader, who has shown us exactly where to place our narrow focus: on the heart.

Without working to change ourselves to narrow our focus to others' hearts, we ultimately risk sacrificing a true relationship with God. When we make a choice to judge and live by physical appearance, we make the decision to reject the goodness and the uniqueness God has created in each and every one of us.

And when we turn away from that uniqueness and that goodness, we miss out on a life of appreciating the most wonderful kind of beauty as molded and formed by the Creator.

# CHAPTER 11

## Putting Down My Shield

As we entered the grocery store, there was a family putting food items into plastic bags from the conveyor belt, and one by one, they turned to watch Brenna. Their little girl, maybe around eight or nine years of age, didn't take her wide eyes off Brenna as we selected a cart and loaded up our kids for our shopping trip.

Out of the corner of my eye, I noticed her getting closer and realized with a quick turn that she was shuffling around us, craning her head to catch another glimpse of our daughter.

In that moment, I froze. Should I say something? And if so, what should I say? And in what tone?

The moment was lost as Evan pushed the cart forward and I, absorbed in my thoughts, followed silently.

And then I was struck with a feeling of helpless guilt: Did I not protect my daughter? While she is young, I am her advocate, her protector. Brenna relies on me to be her defense against the world, a world that does not understand her skin and that, in many cases, does not yet accept visual difference without judgment. And I failed.

It was not the first time we had been met with

openmouthed stares, and it will definitely not be the last. Brenna's skin gives the appearance of a terrible sunburn over her entire body, and with her reddened, peeling skin, shiny with thick lotion, she is frequently the subject of pointing and staring.

From the man at the library who loudly remarked, "That's quite a sunburn!" to the young children who warned each other not to touch Brenna ("You might get it, too"), I am not sure I will ever get used to the reactions. I understand the surprise of seeing noticeable differences, but I don't believe that excuses the disrespect of staring. . .the kind of staring where you intently concentrate on someone's difference instead of looking into her eyes with the respect that we should afford each other as individuals created by the same God.

I have grappled with my own response to the public stares. I struggle with finding the best way to teach kindness and acceptance in a brief encounter with a child at the park or with a gruff old man who asks, "What's wrong with *her*?" Or the people who, unbelievably, actually seem to go out of their way to watch us.

Attending the FIRST National Family Conference in 2014 was, for us, like receiving a warm, understanding hug. We were among strangers, people we had only seen profile pictures of on Facebook, but there was such a comfort among moms, dads, and children. I couldn't figure out why it was so comforting, why I didn't want to even leave the conference until a few days after it ended. I felt physically better at the conference. There was much less tension in my shoulders, my mind was at ease. . .and why?

Because I wasn't on guard for the public reaction. There *was* no public reaction, nothing aside from a smile and hello and kind eyes that said, "Me too, I understand."

During our time with other families whose children also have patchy skin, flaky skin, affected limbs and features, and other differences, I didn't have to be a protector against stares and questions.

One afternoon at the conference, I walked into an open-forum type of discussion greeted by a circle of chairs filled with other mothers eager to talk with, maybe even for the first time, a group who actually empathized and understood. Eventually, inevitably, the topic of public reaction grabbed hold of our group's conversation. Fellow moms shared about experience after experience and feeling after feeling caused by the stares, the pointing, and the questions about their children looking so different from other children.

Eventually, one mother spoke up, a woman named Tracie who had raised her beautiful, successful, confident twenty-eight-year-old daughter, Bailey, as a single mom.

"I used to get so defensive," she told us, recounting experiences of angrily hiding Bailey behind her whenever she would notice people staring at Bailey's skin. "But then I realized something: the more defensive and rude I was with people, the more my daughter hid behind me. I felt like I was protecting her, but I was really drawing more attention to her skin and making her feel ashamed."

Those words are imprinted in my heart now. Because so much of this is not about me and my feelings as a mother.

I am simultaneously teaching people now. I strive to teach the world about my daughter, and I am also teaching my daughter about the world.

I want to explain so many things to strangers—that Brenna almost died when she was born, how much work it is every day to keep her skin comfortable, and most importantly, how she is just another child. I want to be sarcastic and rude when I am met with a ridiculous comment about "letting her" get sunburned. I want to jump to her defense when I notice stares of disgust.

But as time goes on, I see what is much more important than public education about difference: educating Brenna about life, helping her to understand how God sees her and how He created her, and teaching her that her worth and her purpose are found only in God. I want the light of both of my children's differences to shine brightly.

I want my daughter and my son to grow into their teen years and adulthood with confidence and self-assurance. Just as I hope to inspire others to develop empathy as I educate about Brenna's skin, it is also my job to teach my children about empathy and acceptance for others, with the understanding that everyone has challenges in life just as they both do, ranging from family issues to learning disabilities to many other things that make them different but not unworthy or unseen. I want both of my children to learn about kindness and compassion from an early age. . .and this all starts with me and my husband teaching and showing them these things and how they are to do the same for others.

It is my hope that Brenna won't focus on her skin as she grows up because she will be too busy doing all the things that she wants to do—pursuing her own passions, volunteering, studying and reading, displaying kindness to others, and whatever else she feels called to do or has an interest in. Physical appearance can't alter spiritual attributes or personal accomplishments.

But I know she won't learn empathy or selflessness if I am constantly putting up my fists for a fight every time we are in public.

We as parents often want to rush to defend our children. Maybe our daughter is teased for being the smallest in her class, or our son lacks the athletic ability that others on his team possess. Or our child is shunned on the playground for a reason that is completely unclear to us. With every unkind word or snub in the cafeteria or birthday invitation that isn't received, our parental defensiveness boils to the surface. When we feel that someone is rejecting our child, we often feel that rejection deep within ourselves.

Sometimes we need to learn how to stand on a different side instead of rushing to the defense.

One recent day after school, one of my kids exclaimed, "Let's play ring-around-the-rosy!"

So we cleared a small space in the living room, pushing aside the ottoman and a game board set out from the night before. Around and around we spun, the three of us. We chanted the rhyme, we all fell down. . .only to hop back up for another round when someone would say, "Again!"

Then, as we were about to join hands once more, Connor looked at me and said, "I don't want to hold Brenna's hand this time."

I tightened up a bit inside and asked casually, "Why not?"

"Because it's not like yours."

I walked him to another room and gave him a quick, firm, and loving talk about how it's not kind to say that we don't want to hold hands with someone else, especially our sister, and how everyone's hands are different.

"Okay," he said simply.

And yet, again as we started our game, he hesitated to grab hold of his sister's hand.

I became even more upset inside, but as calmly as I could, I took him out of earshot of Brenna again and reminded him that Brenna has special skin and it just feels a little different than Mommy's skin.

This time, he was the one who became frustrated.

"No, Mommy, I'm not talking about her *skin*. I *know* that. She's just not holding my hand right like you do."

Sure enough, when they went to join hands, Brenna grabbed Connor's first two fingers from the front, instead of his whole hand from the back.

It wasn't her skin at all. It was her awkward grip. I had created a whole scene about something that wasn't even an issue, simply because I was making assumptions and jumping on the defense. I failed to see the real issue at hand because I chose to become defensive instead of exploring the heart of the matter.

In sports, they say that defense wins games. On defense, we jump up, on guard against offenders. Every move is against us. Every move is meant to, quite literally, offend us.

But when it comes to relationships with other people, defensiveness doesn't win. In relationships, sometimes we need to put down our shields and realize that not everyone is an offender.

Today, I am learning to let down my guard and avoid looking for battles when we simply want to enjoy a morning at the park or grab a few things at the grocery store. Because I not only want to show my children firsthand what I want them to learn when it comes to how we talk with and approach others, but I also don't think the majority of people are truly attacking. I think there's something deeper, a desire to reach out and somehow express concern, which often comes out as something that seems harsh or intrusive.

When I am asked questions like, "Is that something they're working to clear up?" as if Brenna's severe genetic condition is just acne, it is more natural for me to want to become sarcastic in defense. But these sweet little kids are watching me and listening to me and learning from my responses.

I recently read a definition of grace that said, "Grace is God doing good for us when we don't deserve it." *Doing good, even when we don't deserve it.*

And when God called us to love our neighbors as ourselves, that often means extending that grace that He gives us to those around us—doing good, even when they may not deserve it. It means ignoring the temptation to jump on the defense when others offend, even without necessarily meaning to.

Facing what we perceive as someone's ignorance without grace leads to a growing anger and resentment in our hearts. It leads to defensiveness even when there really is no need to be defensive.

But with grace? Kindness can be mustered up. And

when kindness is extended instead of anger, it builds self-confidence and a heart of contentment.

Grace and forgiveness are two things I struggle with personally; I hold on to things for entirely too long, and sometimes I just have to ask God for months and even years to help me remove anger or resentment in my heart.

But as I have experienced encounter after encounter of different reactions, different questions about Brenna's skin, I have experimented with how I respond and how that makes me feel personally, and most importantly, how that makes my children feel, too.

Many people may not choose the best words to use or convey the kindest facial expression when it comes to approaching us about our daughter. But I know that I sometimes don't make the right or the best choices in my life, either. And yet God still loves me and forgives me. He still gives me grace, an unconditional grace that is even hard to comprehend at times. His grace extends to me kindness when I deserve less. And how much more should I extend kindness and love even, when someone looks at or says something about Brenna?

By giving grace, I don't hold on to ignorant questions as personal insults. My heart is not burdened with anger. I am on the offense, living in joy—not defensive, fists up, ready to pounce on anyone who gives my child a second look. And by giving grace, my children will learn to respond to reactions about Brenna's skin with their heads held high, not hiding in shame and self-doubt.

When Bailey's mom, Tracie, began putting her fists down and instead focused on encouraging her daughter, that did more for her child than almost anything else.

When Bailey was growing up, kids in her school used to call her Scaly Bailey, a horrible nickname to describe the excess flakes of skin on her body due to her ichthyosis…and a nickname that makes me cringe just to type it.

But when I got to meet Bailey as an adult, she absolutely exuded gracefulness. Bailey walks with self-assurance, pursuing passions she has extraordinary talents for, such as dancing and constantly volunteering her time to help children explore interests in the arts.

"Can those questions, whispers, and stares be intrusive? Yes, if we let them," Bailey says. "But we need to be advocates for our differences." She looks at each interaction as an opportunity to teach others about acceptance and to display her unique beauty and pride in the way she was created.

And I believe so much of Bailey's attitude today is because her mom chose grace instead of anger.

Jesus told us to turn the other cheek. Choosing grace doesn't have to mean taking the insults of cruel people without sticking up for ourselves with strength and self-confidence. It may simply look like a dignified response instead of igniting your own firing squad.

And it is my ultimate hope that grace becomes less hard work and more a part of who I am and that with every extension of respect and kindness and compassion, the world will be able to join us in celebrating all kinds of beautiful, however different that may look.

Recently, there was an older gentleman behind us at McDonald's, and he started speaking to me before I was paying attention. I caught something about "keeping a hat on" Brenna, and my face started to get hotter, thinking it was the beginning of a lecture about keeping a hat on my kid when out in the sun so that she doesn't get sunburned (not the first time this has happened).

"What was that?" I asked him, pushing back against my rising defensiveness.

He repeated his comment: "I was just saying that I don't know how you get her to keep a hat on. My grandkids just pull them right off!"

He smiled at us. "She's sure a cutie."

# CHAPTER 12

## Everyone Understands a Smile

W hen I was in middle school, my best friend invited me to dinner with her family.

I always loved spending time with Kristin's family — all eight children and whatever friends who happened to come along and join the fun.

Our reservations for that weekend dinner out, which included several other families, happened to be a destination trip. To an Amish farm.

In 1991, a young boy named Samuel was critically injured on his family's farm when he fell into a tractor-powered drive shaft while doing his farm chores. He sustained such severe injuries—amputating one arm, crushing the other arm, and peeling the scalp from his head—that his survival shocked everyone. . .and with that, his hospital stay and dozens of surgeries racked up hundreds of thousands of dollars in medical bills.

Donations poured in from around the country to help Samuel's family, which included his parents and twelve siblings, and to supplement that, his family began offering sit-down dinners of traditional Amish fare, inviting non-Amish families into their home each week in exchange for a donation to help pay Samuel's medical bills.

All I knew about the Amish before that night was that they dressed in uniform-like, neutral, basic clothing with head coverings for the women and that they didn't use modern amenities.

That evening, their lovely Amish home was warm in contrast to the chilly fall air outside. As the adults conversed deeply across the table after our hearty meal, all of us kids shyly watched each other as we were sprinkled around the living room, dimly lit without electricity. Then eventually, one of their sons asked if we wanted to learn one of their favorite games, opening up both of our groups to casual conversation.

The best part came when the family hitched up a horse and gave us buggy rides around the farm. We all piled in, taking turns and laughing together the way kids do when they are experiencing something fun together, even as strangers.

Different doesn't have to mean strange when we approach strangers with open hearts, despite vastly different cultures, religions, backgrounds, or ways of life. Samuel's family has opened their home to other families around the country for many years, which has been a gift for all involved to be able to learn about and from each other.

"We have learned a great deal from our visitors, and we have tried to tell them something of our way of life,"

Samuel's father, Oba, wrote in a letter to the *Chicago Tribune* in 1996.

"The Golden Rule," he wrote, "is never out of fashion.

"Among strangers, we are always conscious of the fact that we look different from those around us. My feeling has always been that everyone understands a smile."[8]

After that night, the Amish didn't seem so strange. That night, they became, simply, people who chose to live a little differently. They were parents, kids, families who laughed and had fun just like us. That night expanded my understanding of the Amish culture, and still today, I am sure to smile when I see the Amish.

We can decide, every day, how to meet the people around us.

We can choose to compete, to criticize, to compare. Or we can choose to connect.

There are people in our lives where connection comes easily and naturally. We all have relationships in our lives where conversation is easy, we have similar lifestyles and values, we have a lot in common, or we appreciate that person's sense of humor or personality.

And then, there are others in our lives who are more challenging to connect with. Perhaps they have different tactics in disciplining and raising their children, conflicting political or religious views, or polarizing personalities.

---

8. Oba Herschberger, letter to the editor, *Chicago Tribune*, February 4, 1996.

Because of this, our relationships may be strained.

Often, we are naturally inclined to want to criticize that which is different from us. But when we strive to find even just one point of connection with another, that is where we can begin to learn that person's story, to see into his or her heart, to form a deeper connection. It is through that connection that your relationship might flourish. It is through that connection that you can find meaningful beauty in the other person.

When we eye the differences around us with suspicion or with immediate criticism, we are making snap judgments that will strain any connection that can be made. Without them even knowing, we are inviting those people around us into a competition.

When we compare and compete, we divide. When we compare, we either feel less than or greater than—both of which are wrong.

When we compare, we are usually pitting the way we feel about ourselves against the way someone else appears to be. It is unfair to ourselves and to everyone else around us. Painting ourselves as either superior or inferior immediately closes off the chance to make a very real connection with someone else.

But when we connect, we bridge. When we connect, we turn our focus away from ourselves, from appearances, and we look toward another person's heart, to his or her story and feelings and values.

Glennon Doyle Melton, author of *Carry On, Warrior*, once said:

> *Every time we open our mouths and speak, we are either saying "Let there be light" or "Let there be darkness."*
>
> *When we gossip, when we criticize, when we lie or tell hurtful jokes or use labels that categorize and demean people, we are saying "let there be darkness." We create a world around us that is not so beautiful. And then we have to live in it.*
>
> *When we offer a compliment, when we defend a friend or a stranger, when we stick to the truth, when we speak a kind word to anyone, we are saying "Let there be light." We are creating a more beautiful world, and then we get to live in it.*[9]

There is such beauty in cultivating meaningful relationships with those around us—rather than competing, comparing, or criticizing. Instead of going into a conversation with a critical eye or word, how different would the world be if we changed our dialogue to focus on our points of connection—however small or simple they might be—to build our relationships? How different would the world be

9. Glennon Doyle Melton, Instagram post October 2015, Instagram.com/momastery.

if our default was kindness and grace instead of frustration or criticism?

My friend Lauren Casper was dismayed after noticing a trend popping up on blogs and Facebook statuses as letters to fellow mothers that were shaming instead of positive. The most recent she scrolled past was written by a mom who saw a fellow mother with her little girl all dressed up at the park, keeping a very close eye on her daughter—"overprotecting," as the writer was quick to judge.

"I wonder," Lauren muses on her own blog, "if the dreaded mom guilt actually originated as a result of mom judging?"

This writer of this Facebook post knew absolutely nothing about the other family's story, but instead of offering grace and understanding, she put up a wall of comparison and criticism. So Lauren asked instead:

> What if, instead of making assumptions and running
> home to our keyboards, we approached moms at
> the playground with a smile and, "Hi! How old is
> your daughter? She looks so beautiful today!" Or
> after watching mom gasp and rush over to save her
> daughter we offered an understanding smile and said,
> "Playgrounds can be scary, can't they?"
> What doors could be opened and what friendships

*could be forged if we were less attached to our ideas of how other moms should parent and instead were more interested in their stories and their unique family?*

*Because when we're snarky and rude and give disapproving glances, we create walls. So when a mom at the playground might have real questions about parenting styles and tools or the best place to buy shoes that can get wet and dirty she looks around to find walls instead of smiles and open doors.*[10]

Sometimes, we as young kids learn—either directly or subconsciously—to push kindness back as we are encouraged to be "better" than those around us. Kindness begins to evaporate from our actions in favor of success on the sports field, on the stage, in the classroom—the kind of success found in the form of winning at all costs, not the kind of success that lies in doing our best and treating the people next to us with kindness.

Then that mentality continues into adulthood: ACT scores, jobs, parenting, who makes the most money or has the biggest house. Too often, we choose being right or being the best over simply being a good person.

But the Golden Rule should trump everything. Treat

10. Lauren Casper, "Let's Be Careful with Our 'Dear Mom Who' Posts," laurencasper.com (blog), September 26, 2015, http://www.laurencasper.com/2015/09/26/lets-be-careful-with-our-dear-mom-who-_____-posts/.

others the way you would like others to treat you—a principle that reminds us to construct bridges instead of walls with our words and with our actions.

Kindness is a beautiful art that we continually learn to create as we strive to connect with those around us. Love is a whole lot of things, but God makes sure to open His description of love with a reminder that that love is patient and *kind*.

Sometimes, it is fear that keeps us from connecting. Fear of rejection, fear of inferiority, and fear of insecurity can halt any meaningful connection we may be able to make. Even just the desire to avoid the awkwardness of the unknown may hold us back from reaching out.

A few months after Brenna was born, when we were deep in the throes of survival mode after a NICU stay and two more hospitalizations, I heard through mutual friends that a high school classmate of mine had a young son who was diagnosed with cancer: stage IV neuroblastoma.

I didn't cross paths with Claire all that often in high school, but I immediately felt a heart-aching connection to her because both of our children were fighting for their lives.

Less than two months after his diagnosis, Claire's beautiful seventeen-month-old son, Noah, met Jesus in heaven, leaving her and her husband to grapple with their grief and figure out how to make it through each day with

Noah's twin brother. When I saw Noah's obituary in the newspaper, Evan and I decided to attend the visitation. I hadn't seen or talked to Claire in ten years, but I wanted to let her know that I had been praying for their family and to honor Noah's life in that small way.

For a while after the visitation, I worried that maybe Claire had wondered why on earth I had shown up. I hoped that she appreciated our gesture, despite our lack of communication, but wondered if it hadn't been more of an invasion at a very intimately grief-filled time.

Three years after Noah's death, I received a message from Claire, thanking me. "I don't think I told you," she wrote, "but it meant so much to me that you and your husband came to Noah's wake."

Sometimes we push aside connecting because we allow criticism or comparison to take over our hearts first. Other times, we hold back because we don't know how our outreach will be received by others.

Receiving Claire's message was like getting affirmation about the importance of simply saying something, showing up, and putting aside any fears or doubt we may be feeling inside in order to extend ourselves to others in the form of goodwill and compassion.

Writer Anne Lamott, describing a time when her close friends lost their infant son, says in her book *Bird by Bird*, "I automatically think that closing down is safe, but that really staying open and loving is safer, because then we're connected to all that life and love."[11]

Being open to each other keeps us connected. Openness allows no space for walls. Even though it may feel easier to just keep our heads down, finding the courage to look up and meet others is essential to choosing connection over comparison and competition. Sometimes all it takes is a smile.

After all, as I learned from an Amish family as a young kid, everyone understands a smile.

11. Anne Lamott, *Bird by Bird* (New York: Anchor Books, 1995), 190.

# CHAPTER 13

## *"Why Does She Look Like That?"*

The rain drizzled on the campgrounds outside as we pulled up lawn chairs and picnic tables in the modest wood lodge.

An extended family reunion led us to drive cross-country from Illinois to Wyoming when Connor was four and Brenna was two—an ambitious trip that was hectic but unforgettable.

Evan's third cousin sat across the table chatting with us when her seven-year-old daughter plopped into her lap, carefully watching Brenna with a furrowed brow.

"Why does her face look like that?" the little girl asked, without taking her eyes off Brenna.

"That's just how she was born," I replied. "She has very dry skin, so she has to wear really thick lotion to make her skin feel better."

Without hesitation, she responded, *"It's kinda creeping me out."*

I felt it more than I heard it. I felt it deeply in my core, as if someone had shoved the words down my throat and stirred them up in my stomach. The words echoed in my ears, as if she was speaking for the hundreds of other gawking stares we had received up to that point. *Your baby—the one you love more than anything in the world? I don't like the way she looks.*

But her mother stopped the stirring of those words in my stomach almost as quickly as it hit me. Though I am sure she wanted to run in any open direction, she didn't whisk the little girl away in embarrassment. She didn't clamp her hand over the little girl's mouth and shush. She faced the comment headfirst and said her daughter's name with firm admonishment.

"That was extremely rude, and *you know it*. What do you say?"

"I'm sorry." The little girl's head bowed.

They were some of the most unkind words that anyone had ever said directly to me: *"Your daughter's face creeps me out."* And yet, it was handled the best way I've ever experienced a parent dealing with a child's negative comment about Brenna's appearance.

She let her daughter firmly know that saying something negative about someone's appearance was unacceptable. She prompted an apology. And most of all, she was more concerned with how the words might affect us than how they affected her. *She was more troubled with our hurt than her embarrassment.* She didn't let any awkwardness she might have been feeling stand in the way of making her daughter's comment right.

By staying in the situation rather than deserting us, that mother also gave me a chance to explain Brenna's skin just a little more.

By the end of the evening, just a couple of hours later, that same little girl was chasing my little girl and her brother around, showing them photos on her toy camera, and giggling like they'd always known each other.

And then, as she passed by me, that little girl looked at me. In a moment that stood even stiller than the first, with words that echoed far longer in my ears, she said about Brenna, "She's really cute."

I am thankful for that night. It proved to me that out of ignorance, acceptance can be found, can thrive even—that even very unkind words can be made right if we choose to own them, to recognize them, and to correct them. And it proved that as parents, our responsibility to teach kindness and respect to our children takes precedence over personal humiliation caused by their words or actions, every time.

One of the questions I get asked the most is, "How would you prefer people to react to Brenna looking so different?"

My ultimate preference is that people not react at all, actually. On most days, what I truly want is for the questions to stop. What I want is for people to squelch their own curiosity and offer grace to me in the form of "Your daughter is so cute" or "You're doing a great job." I can only dream of a world where we could all learn to extend a little more kindness instead of judgment—a world in which we stand more assured of our place and position in the world and don't have the need to question others (or ourselves).

I like to educate about Brenna's unique appearance when necessary. But I like it even more when those around us look *beyond* her appearance to see her first as a child. How wonderful it is when people simply say hi, comment on how cute both of my kids are, and hold open the door for us at the store or make small talk with us at the park.

Of course, you are curious why Brenna looks the way she does. *"Why is her skin red and peeling? Was she burned?"* Everyone is curious. But kindness and respect should trump curiosity, always.

However, I know that kids are a different story. Kids have no filter. Kids ask questions about everything, and that is how they learn about the world.

If I see a child between the ages of four to eight approaching us, I know a question is coming about Brenna's skin. Children younger than four often don't notice, and children older than eight or nine begin to realize they shouldn't ask about how someone looks directly in front of that person.

Parents seem to be caught by surprise when their children catch a glimpse of Brenna's skin and begin to point, comment, or ask questions. And they have a really difficult time knowing how to answer or respond themselves.

There is the child who immediately points to Brenna at the indoor playground, calling loudly, "Mom, look at *her*!"

His mother quickly hushes him and tells him, "Come here," where she whispers what I only assume is some kind of reprimand.

There is the older child at the end of the same grocery store aisle as we are who catches a glimpse at the baby in my cart and turns to ask his mom, "Why is that baby so red?" Without looking back, she practically clamps a hand over his mouth, pulling him around the corner.

And there is the family of kids who freeze, staring openmouthed at my daughter at the library, with the mother who gets a rising panic in her eyes as she tries to distract them to look anywhere but at us.

I recognize all of this unfolding, nearly every day. I hear all the questions, I glimpse all the pointing out of the corner of my eye, and I notice all the whispered comments. I feel it all—this questioning and pointing at my daughter's appearance—deep within my heart.

And then the whole situation is, for me, made much worse when parents then try to hide it.

And here's what I want to say: You're embarrassed, and I understand that. But when you try to hide these obvious conversations that are happening right in front of us, it feels like you're hiding from our family. It feels like the small, insignificant gap between us that your child has noticed has now grown into a wide-spanning canyon that no one wants to cross.

I wish you would close that small gap by relating to us as you would to any other family on the playground, instead of making the gap bigger by treating us as unapproachable.

When your child points and tells you to look, I wish you would respond clearly, "Yes, look at that little girl. It looks like she's having so much fun playing, just like you are!"

When your child asks you, "Why is that baby so red?" or "Why does she look like that?" I wish you would answer honestly: "I'm not sure, but the way someone looks isn't important. We all look different from each other, don't we? Just like you have curly hair and I have straight hair!"

I wish you would encourage your child to say hi and to ask my kids' names.

I wish you would apologize without feeling ashamed if your child is offensive right in front of us: "I'm so sorry; we're still learning how to ask questions respectfully." It also goes a long way if you tack on: "Your daughter is so cute. How old is she?"

And above all, I wish you would proactively talk about differences more often with your children. I wish you would read children's books about being different, and I wish you would positively and naturally converse about various kinds of differences—from wheelchairs to birthmarks, Down syndrome to skin disorders, and racial differences to wearing glasses.

Ultimately, I hope all our children learn that if they have questions about someone's appearance, they can ask you later, privately, so they don't hurt anyone's feelings—because, after all, how we treat each other is much more important than how someone looks.

I wish you wouldn't hide. I wish you would leave these conversations about us, in front of us, open so that we can join in if we want to, instead of running away because you're embarrassed. As much as you might want the ground to swallow you up when your child looks at mine, points, and exclaims, "Look how red she is!" there is nothing to be scared of. . .and when you act afraid to be around us, it teaches your children that Brenna is scary because she's different.

That doesn't mean coming directly up to us and asking questions about Brenna's appearance simply because you're curious. Questions can be tiring, and when they come from adults, it can feel especially intrusive. That also doesn't mean going out of your way to "use" our family as your real-life example of the boy in the young adult novel *Wonder*. We want to teach our children that we are *all* different, not that Brenna is the "different one" simply because her appearance is noticeably unusual.

Some people in the disabled community say that they are not here to be a learning opportunity for others. But I would argue that we are *all* constant learning opportunities for everyone else, and especially for children—by our actions, our words, and the way we treat each other and ourselves. And with that quick point and question, we as parents are given a choice: to either teach how to avoid or be embarrassed around people with disabilities, or to help our kids learn that everyone was awesomely and uniquely created by God, in all shapes, sizes, and colors.

Instead of a steep divide that places our family on the other side with a Do Not Look at and Do Not Talk to sign, I'd rather be a positive opportunity for your child to learn how to respect and appreciate physical differences.

And I believe that once we start treating people with disabilities and differences as we do anyone else, we will help our children realize that indeed they are just like anyone else—each of us created by our great God as a different beautiful.

# CHAPTER 14

## Accepting Beautiful in Your Life

Because of the way it grows quickly, building tightly upon itself, Brenna's skin is very restrictive, especially if it gets dry. It took nearly a year for her to be able to completely open her fingers, which were formed into clenched fists at birth, fingers encased in what looked like hard plastic caps.

In her early months, if her fingers, toes, or limbs were stretched beyond their limited flexibility, the skin would break open, leaving painful cracks around her joints. It is easy to take for granted how pliable our skin is, stretching flexibly to accommodate all kinds of movement. Brenna's skin does not stretch like this.

And when your skin doesn't stretch, you don't want to move much, affecting your joints and muscles in the process. Movement has come slowly for Brenna, with her first steps shortly after her second birthday and crawling that occurred at twenty-seven months.

Brenna hates to feel off balance and lacks the muscle strength that allows her to catch herself if she falls. Physical contact like bumps and pushes, and especially cuts and scratches, can be hurtful to her body.

So Brenna takes life slowly.

Anyone who takes her hand to cross a parking lot can expect to shuffle slowly along with each of her careful steps. Stepping over a crack or threshold will take several seconds as she musters her courage and balance.

But what this has given Brenna is a true attention to detail. She is not very concerned with what is ahead but more so what the next step will be like. She is paying attention to what is happening right now.

Because she is moving slowly, she sees the bird that lands on the sidewalk, gleefully pausing to call out, "Hi, birdie!" Because she is not running quickly, she notices the truck that just went by, explaining that it looked like "Daddy's truck." And in the middle of the rush of school, she slowly takes in the activity, reporting on what color shirts her friends were wearing that day.

We are programmed to look toward the next. But Brenna reminds me about the need to seize our ability to notice the little things as we live each day—grabbing at life's moments instead of forcing life to grab us in order to get us to slow down because we aren't paying attention. At least, we're not paying attention to the *now*. And the *why* and the *how*. We're too busy living in the "what's next," anticipating instead of appreciating.

But there is so much beauty the world has to offer us if we take the opportunity to accept it. It's not the kind of beauty found in the cover models on magazines or the colorful new kitchen appliances in the Sunday ads but rather the pieces of different beautiful, large and tiny, that have been created for us, outside of our window and within our own hearts. Often we don't even need to seek out this different beautiful but simply to turn our heads to see things from a new angle, to realize this different beautiful is right in front of us or right next to us, there for the taking.

All of these surprising kinds of beautiful are God's loving gifts to us. And accepting these pieces of beautiful is our gift back to God, as a way to honor and glorify Him.

The offer is on the table, every day—what the world has to offer us, what our different life experiences have to offer us, what our bodies have to offer us. And it's our choice to accept, to reach out and grasp these offerings, to hold on tightly as cultural trends and ideas challenge what we believe and know.

As we accept God's version of beautiful in our lives through all we experience and see, we must continually redefine this beauty, accepting it time and time again.

Each of us, in different ways, can always be better. But finding beauty in who we are, both inside and outside, also means being content with how incredible we are, right now, instead of endeavoring to be better and to become more.

In a world that tells us "You're not enough. . .go be more," truly liking ourselves is a rebellious act. Actually calling ourselves beautiful is almost considered arrogant or conceited. Accepting a compliment with a beaming, gracious thank-you instead of protesting is far too uncommon.

But if we're not enough for ourselves, how can anything else be enough for us?

If we can't accept the beautiful that God has placed within us, how can we fully accept the beautiful that God has placed around us?

Wanting to look our best isn't necessarily what's wrong with society; it's in wanting to look someone else's best where we become trapped.

I think that self-awareness and self-acceptance help to rid us of our insecurities. Secure people do not feel the need to compete, compare, and criticize. Secure people are much more likely to simply want to connect.

And how do we build security within ourselves? By learning who we are and learning to like ourselves.

Too often, we hold on to such specific expectations or false perceptions of exactly what various parts of our lives should be or should look like. Sometimes we even ignore what we actually *like* in favor of the shoulds and the supposed-tos.

And that is what our children see day after day. That is what our kids learn as they watch us and absorb the way they should think and act. We tell our children to "be themselves" and to "be confident in who they are," and then we turn around and live in self-doubt and place unrealistic expectations on ourselves.

If we are going to be the difference makers in changing our children's world to a different kind of beautiful, it starts with consistency from us—in what we think, what we say, but mostly how we act.

It starts with an acceptance of the beauty that life is offering us. It starts with seeing that magnificence and wonder right in front of us, right within us, and finding the courage to celebrate that, despite the world around us telling us that we shouldn't like ourselves, that we are supposed to be a certain way and look a certain way to be truly beautiful and wonderful.

Sometimes, it simply starts with showing up.

In 2014, a team of surgeons removed two-thirds of my friend Michele's tongue and rebuilt it with tissue from her arm and her thigh.

Michele had received her second diagnosis of mouth cancer and had undergone multiple surgeries and treatments in three short years. All this for a dynamic, outgoing woman and mother of six who makes her living as none other than a speaker.

For years, Michele built up a speaking career that took her all over the country, sharing her wisdom and voice with women's groups and conferences. After these invasive mouth surgeries, Michele wondered if her career as a speaker might be over.

"How would I read a book to my children before bed, let alone address hundreds or thousands from a stage?" she writes on her blog, MicheleCushatt.com. "No one wants to listen to speaker who can't talk, right?"[12]

Following her diagnoses, treatments, and surgeries, Michele struggled through hours and hours of speech therapy and oral exercises and stretches, forcing her mouth to form words through immense pain. And through all of this, the uncertainty of her career nagged her deeply.

All of these questions gave way to a big temptation for Michele: to hide. To shut her door to her career and online platform forever.

"The prospect of putting myself back out there again—scarred, altered, different—terrified me. And shamed me. I was embarrassed of my new self, and I didn't want anyone to see what I'd become," she says.

But then Michele stepped out. After months and months of intensely painful recovery, she began to speak again.

She first spoke at three weekend services at a church in Colorado, followed by new coaching gigs for speaking clients, and then another two speeches in front of five hundred women in Chicago. Finally, she flew to Nashville to

12. Michele Cushatt, "The Sweet Success of Showing Up," michelecushatt .com (blog), September 24, 2015, http://michelecushatt.com/the-success-of -showing-up/.

cohost the widely popular *This Is Your Life* podcast with Michael Hyatt—*thirteen* thirty-minute podcasts over the course of two days.

What she discovered during this time was what she had been wondering all those months: she was not the same speaker as she once was. She sounds different, sometimes she spits, and she struggles with words that used to come easily.

But Michele also discovered something else, something unexpected. She realized that her personal success has been misunderstood.

> *If my goal is to speak with perfection, to be the articulate woman I was before, then I am finished. That option is no longer on the table. But success isn't displayed on a stage or in obvious demonstrations of perfection. Real success is the battle you fight and win inside. When you muster the courage to face down the very thing you fear most. To square your shoulders, take a deep breath, and run hard toward it when everything in you wants to run away.*[13]

The first weeks that Michele took the stage once again, stepped up to the microphone once again, and even sat in front of a video camera once again were extremely difficult—but they were also extremely beautiful.

13. Cushatt, "The Sweet Success of Showing Up."

That beauty was revealed in the ability to let others truly see her, and in doing so, "to discover I'm loved, exactly as I am," she says. "To do what I love to do, even as a broken and changed [woman], and find the darkness also surprisingly full of light."

She looked up and found this new kind of beauty, this new kind of accomplishment that was being offered to her. And instead of hiding, she accepted it. She discovered that her success is no longer about performance but instead about showing up.

> *If you've experienced a setback, don't be surprised when you feel the temptation to hide—to slink back into a corner and avoid exposing yourself to risk once again. It's to be expected, and it's certainly an option. Or you can fight for your life. You can face down your fear and allow yourself to be seen, as you are. You can do what you love and, at the same time, turn a deaf ear to performance-driven definitions of success.*

Michele was offered a new truth that she began to embrace and accept: "Showing up requires far more courage than showing off."[14]

Being who we are, with all our glorious imperfections, is an opportunity that we are always offered, but that can be so easy to turn away from, to hide from.

14. Cushatt, "The Sweet Success of Showing Up."

Why do we shy away from hard?

Going off the trail means a lot of rough terrain and many unknowns. But this is where the truly indescribable beauty often lies. . .just beyond the easy path.

God is offering so much wondrous beauty to us, but it starts within and is often found in the very hard. Do we have the courage to slow our rush so that we may recognize the magnificence within us and in front of us? Do we have the bold audacity to accept that kind of beautiful so that we can truly learn to celebrate the wondrous beauty that is spilling over into our lives?

# CHAPTER 15

## From the Inside Out

*F*or three years, a tiny opening gave Brenna life.

That opening was a lifeline for nourishment that we used month after month to be able to give Brenna's body the large amount of food and liquid that she needs to live and to grow.

For reasons we still don't know—although we all have different theories—Brenna's consumption began to drop steadily the summer after she was born. She began to drink from her bottle less and less, as we frantically tried anything we could think of with the guidance of a feeding therapy team. . .feeding at different inclines, burping her more or less often, trying the milk a little cooler or a little warmer.

After multiple hospitalizations for dehydration and weeks of weight loss, Evan and I made the desperate decision to have a gastronomy feeding tube, also called a g-tube, placed in her stomach.

Unfortunately, this tube never gave us the relief that was promised to us. Tube-feeding caused all kinds of stress for our family, from constant vomiting to the frustrations of working a feeding pump in a restaurant during a day trip out of town. And because she was so full from being essentially force-fed through her tummy, Brenna stopped eating by mouth altogether, and we grieved the loss of this important life skill.

However, for all our work to learn how to work a feeding pump and to learn how to blend up food to push into her stomach, Brenna began to gain weight. She began to grow. And she stayed out of the hospital.

When she was close to two years old, we began to feel that it was time for her to eat on her own. We embarked on a journey to wean her from her tube—a journey that consumed months of her life but that led victoriously to Brenna eating and drinking completely by mouth once again. It was a success swirled with relief and joy that we celebrated every single day when we could sit down to dinner together as a family or when we could have a picnic outdoors without a feeding pump sharing the picnic blanket.

Eventually, after a year of that little button sticking out of her stomach unused, we were encouraged by our feeding team to remove it.

So that lifeline was taken out, and Brenna underwent a basic procedure to close the tiny little hole in her tummy that wasn't closing on its own as most tend to do, like an earring hole.

But as we sat in church on the Sunday morning following her surgery, I noticed the front of her dress was wet.

Although she was always very careful and clean, I reasoned that surely she must have just spilled some of her water from her sippy cup.

A look at her surgical site when we got home showed a tiny indent directly in the middle where it had been perfectly lined and stitched just hours before.

And within a few hours, her tiny hole had completely opened up, growing each time we checked it until stomach contents were oozing out and we could easily see the layers into her stomach. Brenna was admitted into the children's hospital that evening.

The fact that her first surgery failed was unusual, and the surgeons went over several options over the next day with us. Finally, it appeared as if the next step would be a much more invasive procedure, where they would need to open up her stomach even more in order to find better tissue to stitch up.

The first few days of recovery were rough. Brenna was in a great deal of pain, she wasn't allowed to eat for several days, she couldn't shake a high fever, and her usually good skin care was suffering in the hospital setting.

And then our hearts sank when, five or six days after her second, bigger surgery, the stitches began to pull apart again.

Each day, Brenna's surgical incision opened just a little bit more, like a zipper from one side to the other.

The one thing that gave us hope was that her stomach layers and her muscle layers all seemed to be completely intact still. But her skin layers were struggling to stay closed and to heal.

From the beginning, Brenna's surgeon reassured us that wounds in our bodies heal "from the inside out." She acknowledged that Brenna's incision opening was not ideal, but she continued to believe that it was healing from the inside well and that healing would work its way out.

We were, thankfully, discharged from the hospital eight days later so that Brenna could heal at home, but we watched and reported back to her doctors about that pesky incision each day.

And then one morning, we woke up to find that Brenna's tummy had changed its course. The opening had gotten smaller.

Almost before our eyes, the healing had reached the outside from within. Brenna's super skin-making abilities then kicked into gear, and the zipper-like incision began to close.

Before long, that opening that had caused everyone so much concern had become a thin line of a scar across her little tummy, just in time for her to start her new year of preschool.

We tended to that little spot on Brenna's tummy not only for those two scary weeks but each day for the three years that her tube resided in her stomach. And as I peered discerningly at that opening each day after her surgery, I marveled at the glorious way God created the human body to work, to heal from the inside out.

As a wound begins to heal, the basic connective tissue of the skin collagen expands into that wound area, creating a foundation that supports the rebuilding of the skin.

When that framework is in place, the network of blood vessels migrates to it, and with the increased blood supply to nourish it, skin and nerve cells begin to form from the bottom up. Healing from the inside out.

Until Brenna's surgery, I was unaware that the body works in this way. But it is not surprising God formed us like this, because He also works within our hearts in exactly the same way.

First Thessalonians tells us that God created us to have a spirit, soul, and body, and, according to Philippians, God works in us to do His good purpose. God wants to change us from the inside out.

When we give our lives to Jesus as Lord, God moves within us, giving us eternal life with Him. God lives within us, allowing us to live as Jesus taught us to live—serving each other, loving each other. When we choose to allow God into ourselves, we open our spirits and souls to His great love, and we can bring that great love to the world.

First John 4:4 reminds us, "The one who is in you is greater than the one who is in the world."

If we allow the outside in, instead of pouring out God's great love from the inside out, healing can't happen. Just as an outside infection interferes with the healing of a wound, the negative influences from the outside world can prolong our soul's healing and can interfere with us carrying out God's work inside us.

Several years ago, I heard author, speaker, and human trafficking activist Christine Caine speak about the way that God worked intensely within David for a very long time before he was strong enough and capable enough to fulfill his calling as king and share God's light from within to his people.

To elaborate on her message, Christine used the analogy of a darkroom, which really struck a chord with me, being a photographer. What she said was this:

*In a darkroom, we must be very careful with the film, because if it is not properly cared for and if light touches it before the chemicals that create the picture are done, the picture will be destroyed.*

*God works in us a lot more like a roll of film than a quick upload to Instagram. So we need to go into the darkroom with God, a place of obscurity and anonymity, and let Him work in our hearts so that*

*His image is in us. Because if the light of God within
us is not greater than the light of the world outside,
the outside world will destroy us.*[15]

In the Bible, 2 Corinthians 4:6 reveals: "For God, who said, 'Let light shine out of darkness,' made his light shine in our hearts to give us the light of the knowledge of God's glory displayed in the face of Christ."

The light must hit our hearts before we can project it out into the world. God must work inside us first before we can share His work with others around us. Just as our bodies get better from the inside out so that we can be healed and strengthened, our hearts do the same.

"God's not looking for more shooting stars; he's looking for more lighthouses," Christine Caine said.

Shooting stars seem brilliant at first glance, but they are short lived; these streaks of light in the dark sky burn up as soon as they hit the earth's atmosphere. Lighthouses, on the other hand, have a strong illumination from within that they project outward, lighting the way for others.

For weeks, I watched the noticeable scar across Brenna's stomach pull itself closed, witnessing firsthand how our bodies heal from the inside out.

It is the same with our spirits and our souls, so that we can be God's lighthouses, fulfilling our wonderful

15. Christine Caine, speech, She Speaks Conference, July 2014.

purposes by first allowing God to move within us, in His darkroom untouched by the infection and influence of the outside, and then shining that light of the good works of our masterful Creator for all to be healed and strengthened by.

# CHAPTER 16

## Acceptance without Pity Means True Understanding of Different

*I* hear you say it as you pass by us at the home-improvement store.

I hear you say it when ending a brief conversation about why my daughter's skin looks the way it does.

I hear your child say it after she questions, wide eyed, what is on my daughter's face.

And I hear you say it as you watch my daughter slowly but determinedly climb up the playground steps.

"Aww. *Poor thing.*"

But you are teaching my daughter something tragic with this statement. What you are conveying to her when she hears you expressing this kind of pity is that she *is* a poor thing. That she is pitiful.

And as she grows older, if she continues to receive this tragic response, she will start to believe it. She will believe that people feel sorry for her, and she will believe she is less than. She may even believe that her life is not a good one, not as good as those who have "normal" skin.

What is pity? Pity is the feeling of sorrow caused by the suffering and misfortunes of others.

Brenna is not suffering. She has periods of hurt and of discomfort, and she has endured intense pain during hospitalizations and surgeries. But on a daily basis, she is not suffering; she is thriving and happy.

She might tell you otherwise, particularly when she doesn't get her way. If you listen to her tantrums when we put chicken pot pie in front of her at dinnertime instead of pizza, you might think she's suffering.

But when people feel sorry for her, she might be inclined to believe that she lives a sad life. Which is completely untrue.

My friend Mary Evelyn's son Simeon was born with spina bifida and is unable to walk, so he pushes himself in a wheelchair (and has been masterfully maneuvering his chair since he was just eleven months old!).

Simeon's wheelchair has unfortunately proven to be the elephant in the room when Mary Evelyn takes him out to the library or to the grocery store. What everyone sees is the chair, not her son.

And while the adults awkwardly avoid talking about his wheelchair, children ask pointed questions: "Why is he in that?" and "Why can't he walk?" and "Will he need it forever?" But for Mary Evelyn, the questions are easy. Questions have answers, and she can easily explain that Simeon's legs aren't strong enough to walk, just as our family can explain that Breanna was born with skin that looks a little different.

But one day, Mary Evelyn watched as Simeon turned in circles outside the sanctuary after church and was approached by a smiling little girl, maybe six years old. She placed herself right in front of Simeon and without taking her eyes from his face, she declared, "I feel sorry for him."

Mary Evelyn admitted:

*I felt it like a kick in the ribs. "I feel sorry for him" is not a question. It is a statement of fact. A revelation. A public disclosure of something I know to be true. Although I fight against it and try to believe otherwise, I know there are many, many people who feel the same. Many people see my son, smiling and spinning and exploring his world, and they feel sorry. They feel sadness. But adults know how to filter. We know what not to say. We know to bottle up.*

This little girl was a leak in the system, Mary Evelyn realized. A system that tells her that Simeon's wheelchair is something to be saddened by. A system that uses words like *confined to*, *suffers from*, and *bound*.

"A system that prefers to see people like my son as victims, as recipients of charity, as less-fortunates waiting to be healed, rather than seeing them as neighbors, colleagues, teachers, and friends," Mary Evelyn writes on her blog *What Do You Do, Dear?* "I wanted so desperately to undo the damage done by a system that is still learning to accept my son."[16]

---

16. Mary Evelyn Smith, "A Leak in the System: When a Little Girl Felt Sorry for My Son," *What Do You Do, Dear?* (blog), July 11, 2014, http://www.whatdoyoudodear.com/a-leak-in-system-when-little-girl-felt/.

Not only does this kind of pity teach our children that they are indeed pitiful, I suspect and fear that they may begin to realize that others see them as less fortunate—and use that to their advantage in a negative way.

With pity sometimes comes special treatment. The characters in John Green's popular novel *The Fault in Our Stars* referred to it as "cancer perks." Those fictional teens in the book were both undergoing treatment for cancer and joked with each other about the special ways that people went out of their way to fulfill any need or desire simply because they had cancer.

One day I wrote on my blog about Brenna being in the throes of threenagerdom. If you're not familiar with this very appropriately created word, a *threenager* is a three-year-old who often exhibits the behavior of a teenager—overly dramatic, sassy, excessively opinionated or know-it-all, emotional, and irrational. Any and all of the above.

Connor made it through the twos and the threes just fine. Brenna, on the other hand, hit three years old and became a Sour Patch Kid commercial—insane and irrational one minute and loving and sweet the next.

I described on my blog, with a mix of frustration and humor, this new stage we had hit, and a woman commented, "With all that she has been through, I would be grateful no matter how she acted."

And yet this is a well-intentioned but very harmful way

of thinking, and another variation of pity.

To parent with this frame of thinking only serves to enable bad behavior using the justification that our daughter deserves to act poorly or disobey because she has a medical condition.

But Brenna is fully capable of behaving, of listening and obeying. Her skin is not an excuse for poor behavior, and to show her favor in this way would be to show her pity as our child: *I feel bad for you, so I am letting you act in this manner that would not be acceptable if you didn't have this skin condition.*

What a disservice this would be to her, and what a detriment to our entire family dynamic, if we let our daughter act however she wanted because we felt sorry for her "for all that she's been through," while holding our son to different standards.

Perhaps the next time we feel sorry for someone, we need to stop and question why. Is it because that person is different than we are? Is it because that person doesn't have something that we have? Is it because that person is enduring a hardship that we haven't had to endure?

Then maybe, instead of projecting pity, we can start learning to transform that feeling of sorry into a feeling of respect and of admiration.

Instead of saying, "Poor thing," what if someone instead said to our daughter, "You're a strong girl!"

Because she is. And not because she lives with this condition. Brenna knows no different. But she is strong because she faces her fears. She is strong because of the courage she shows when she is so nervous before surgery. She is strong because of her self-awareness, knowing and expressing when she is feeling too hot or when her skin is too dry and needs lotion. She is strong because she struggles with the activities that her peers can easily do but doesn't give up.

Those things aren't pitiful at all. They're admirable.

I received a message one day from a woman who shared some of her own story with me, saying that her perspective as a parent of a typical child was starting to shift after reading about Brenna and our family. At first glance, it appeared to be the kind of message that I receive often, where a reader says something along the lines of, "I realized that I have nothing to complain about after seeing what Brenna has endured," a message that sometimes has the undertones of pity. But pity was nowhere to be found in this e-mail.

This woman explained that she had gone through unexplained infertility and had eventually gotten pregnant through in vitro fertilization. But though it was cause for celebration, her pregnancy was also traumatic as she was overcome with stress that she might experience loss.

She gave birth to a healthy baby girl but sank into postpartum depression during a difficult recovery from a C-section, and the pain medication greatly decreased her milk supply, causing her to feel again like a failure.

"I spent many hours crying in secret, trying to sort out

my emotions from hormones, having very dark thoughts, regretting wanting to have children at all," she wrote me. She began to read blogs from other mothers, finding encouragement and hope in the stories.

> *As my daughter grew older, became a little less of a handful, and my moods began to improve, I found something else through your stories: appreciation. I began to appreciate my child. Appreciate the fact that, now at eleven months, she can crawl and babble, and pull herself up to reach and explore new things. Appreciate that I can take her to daycare and know she has fun during the day while I go to work. Appreciate that she eats meatloaf and mashed potatoes in big bites and stuffs cheerios into her mouth with both hands. Appreciate her happy ten-minute splashes in the tub before bedtime. Appreciate, simply, that she is happy and healthy.*

And as she learned how to find this kind of appreciation, this woman also began to learn how to adjust some of her views of parenthood.

> *I had always thought that, as a mom, my job is to teach my child not to be rude to those who are disabled or different, not to point or jeer or bully. But, having read stories like yours, I now realize it's so much more than that. Instead of teaching her to turn and look away, I should explain to her*

*that difference is something to be embraced, not ignored. There is so much difference in the world, and I would be failing her if I didn't show her how to see the beauty in variety, and celebrate them accordingly.*

*My husband and I are now expecting a second child, a little miracle conceived naturally, unexpectedly. I hope that this time I will take that appreciation with me from the beginning, and that one day I can teach both my children to see people like Brenna and know, truly, that beauty comes in every form.*

This woman gave me a gift as she recounted her experiences. Instead of seeing our daughter as someone to be pitied, she found appreciation for all that Brenna is accomplishing and for the way that has changed our family's hearts, and in that, she discovered appreciation for many pieces of her own life as well.

She didn't view our daughter as a "poor thing" who "has it so much worse than me." She did not express sadness for our family and use that to build herself up. Instead, she began to learn that we can all find appreciation and admiration for the different beautiful around us, no matter the circumstances.

When we pity, we remove the opportunity to appreciate. We reject the opportunity to admire the beautiful that can be found in these differences.

But beauty does indeed come in every form.

# CHAPTER 17

## Puzzle Pieces

The path to motherhood was not what my friend Ginger expected at all as she and her husband, Chance, dreamed of having a baby. They mourned together through three miscarriages and one failed domestic adoption before starting paperwork to adopt internationally.

Where they could have limited themselves to their perception of what their family "should" look like, they instead made the decision to follow God's limitless plan for them as He began to piece their family together.

Ginger has always been an advocate for the special-needs community, tutoring mentally disabled students in the special-needs department of her high school and beginning a career as a developmental therapist. But it was her husband who first felt a divine call to adopt a special-needs child.

When they received the paperwork for their potential son, a five-year-old boy from a Bulgarian orphanage, Chance and Ginger wavered in their decision. Nasko had many delays and an uncertain future. They were told that he could potentially thrive in a loving home but that it was also possible that he'd never live independently.

In the orphanage, Nasko was seen as a nuisance, especially because of his special needs. He had feeding issues, which meant he struggled to take a bottle and required vigilant attention as he ate solid foods. He didn't communicate verbally, so he would impulsively go after anything he wanted without a thought to his own safety or the safety of the other orphans.

Nasko was rarely compliant, was extremely active, and was frustrated by the inconsistency of the rules from one adult to the next. Ginger and Chance eventually discovered that his behaviors and inability to fall in line made him an easy target for exhausted and angry orphanage workers.

But they prayed as they pored over his medical history and the detailing of his special needs, and they felt God whispering, *"He may not have been a child you would have chosen, but he is the child I have chosen for you."* Ginger recalls,

*When my husband first felt those words in his core, he wrote them on a scrap of paper and pressed it into my hand. In that moment, I was on the phone with our adoption agency and was trying to analyze and predict what a future with Nasko might look like. But after God whispered to my husband, the statistics, the needs, the delays, and the behaviors—they no longer mattered. God, the Father to the Fatherless, celebrated my future son's life as beautiful.*[17]

A couple of years after bringing Nasko home from Bulgaria, in a surprising turn of events, Ginger became pregnant with their son Louis. And soon, after giving birth, God moved in their hearts again to adopt for a second time, choosing for them another special-needs son from Latvia.

For a time when their children included just Nasko and Louis, Chance and Ginger were planning to move to Sierra Leone, Africa, to be closer to Chance's ministry work. But then Chance was asked to stay in the United States because his fund-raising work was so effective, helping to financially support the African-based ministry, Lifegate International. A few days later, they received word that a little boy with special needs from Latvia was available for adoption. The puzzle was falling into place, and Edward was placed into their family, completing a missing part of their picture.

With each addition—first marriage, then the adoptions and birth of their sons—Ginger and Chance's family formed a more complete, more beautiful, picture. For two of their sons, with a nudge from God, Chance and Ginger fought to show the world that those two beautiful boys belonged perfectly in their family, that they have so much

17. Ginger Newingham, "What Actually Matters: A Guest Post by Ginger Newingham," *Blessed by Brenna* (blog), August 7, 2015, http://www .courtneywestlake.com/celebrating-beautiful-what-actually-matters-by -ginger-newingham/.

to offer, despite their uncertain beginnings marked with neglect.

One of my favorite authors, Jen Hatmaker, wrote in an e-mail to her subscribers:

> *We really can be for each other and learn to hold the tension in areas we are different. I'm dying for more people to commit to holding tension instead of dropping the line, which is easier, sure, but the losses outweigh the relief.*
>
> *You know what people want more than anything? To belong. What if we were more committed to belonging together than being right over each other? I don't want your rightness; I want your presence.*[18]

We may be changed and transformed—physically, mentally, emotionally—throughout our journey of life. And we should be. But we still all *belong*. We always have something exceptional to offer—even the exceptional of the simple is still cause for celebration. Even the exceptional of the mundane belongs richly in the world.

Piecing together puzzles has always been something our son, Connor, excels at; his brain just works that way.

18. Jen Hatmaker to E-mail Friends mailing list, September 15, 2015, http://us8.campaign-archive1.m/?u=d0273e3d2b1973ce522de7c95&id=6dc337c51c&e=fc7fe9ce99.

The comprehension on his face is discernable as he concentrates on figuring out where each piece joins with another within the emerging picture.

The night before Connor started preschool, I crafted a letter to him as I prepared to send him away from home for the first time. Though it was just nine short hours each week, I knew it was the beginning of his true independence. . .the beginning of influence by people other than me and Evan, especially his peers. The beginning of me letting go and letting Connor make his own decisions and find his own way in life.

And so I wrote these words to him:

*Do you know how much people are like puzzle pieces, Connor? Everyone has a different shape. . .a different color. . .a different appearance.*

*But we all fit together in the big picture. We can all come together to make something complete, to make something beautiful.*

*Everyone has their own place in this life, a space and a purpose specifically carved out for them by our awesome God.*

*Some fit in the middle, with bright colors and others on all sides of them. And some are outsiders, joining together with just a couple of other pieces on the edge of the picture. But we still need those so-called outsiders, you see, to make the puzzle work. There is a place for everyone, for every piece, in this big world.*

*You will spend a lot of time trying to find your place in the puzzle. With each activity that you participate in, each interest you pursue, each subject that you study, each friend that you make, you will be creating your own path, seeking your place in the puzzle.*

*Just remember, Connor, that everyone else is trying to find their own place in the puzzle too. Some won't fit into certain parts of the picture that you will, and you won't fit into certain parts that others will. And that's okay. There is a place for everyone, and everyone is important in building the puzzle.*

*So please know that you don't need to try to change your shape to fit in. You are who you are, and you are important. You are special, and you are loved. You are you. I hope you always strive to better yourself as a person, but don't conform just to try to fit in.*

*Be proud of who you are, what you look like, what you like, and all of the important things you have to offer the world. And help others be proud of these things too, by accepting both their similarities and differences. If someone doesn't fit next to you on the puzzle, that doesn't mean they don't belong—everyone will make an important impact on the big picture.*

*So tomorrow, as you leave our house to make new friends and learn new things, I pray that you will always treat others with kindness. That you will try to include instead of exclude. And that you will always listen to your heart when it tells you what the right thing to do is.*

I knew that because he was a three-year-old, most of this analogy would be lost in his sweet young mind. But as he grows older, my hope is that these words will begin to click—the first time he gets teased. The first time he feels inclined to tease. The first time he sees someone else being ostracized. And if not the first time, then the second, third, or fourth. Because this concept will be tested and challenged again and again throughout life. And sometimes it takes a lot of reinforcement to help someone realize how essential *everyone* is to the bigger picture. Sometimes it is a process to fully know and acknowledge how much everyone has to offer, how much everyone truly belongs.

Several years after I wrote that letter, Connor and I pulled out several puzzles to complete on a lazy Saturday afternoon.

He chose a forty-eight-piece puzzle first, a scene from the movie *Frozen* with a dancing Olaf front and center. He pulled out the pieces on top of our breakfast bar, getting them all right side up and in place to start while I finished unloading the last of the dishwasher.

We worked quickly together, arms overlapping as we slid the pieces into place, offering, "Nice job!" when one of us would solve a particularly tricky area. As we came down to the finish, it was clear that the numbers didn't add up—those four spots left couldn't be filled with the three remaining pieces.

I scoured the countertop, lifting the box and pushing school papers out of the way in my search. Connor popped in the last three pieces and looked at the puzzle with dismay.

It's easy to forget how much of an impact that one tiny piece makes when it goes missing. That open spot looks so forlorn, so incomplete.

Finally we found the missing piece on the floor under the table. And our picture was complete. Every piece was in its place where it belonged.

But then we came to another puzzle—a *Toy Story* picture with a large image of Buzz Lightyear with his alien pals.

As we pieced together the last few yet again, I looked in the container and spotted another piece. But when I went to pull it out, Connor reminded me, "No, that's an extra, remember? There are two pieces with Buzz's eye."

An extra piece. I held it as Connor placed the last of

the alien pieces into their spots on the puzzle, forming a completed picture. There was no spot for the second piece of Buzz Lightyear's eye; the puzzle was solved. Finished.

And there's really no place for two of anyone else in this world, either. It takes just one of us to complete the big, beautiful puzzle. Replicating someone else would just leave the picture with an extra—an extra that the big picture doesn't need.

Ginger's sons Nasko and Edward both have severe ongoing mental and physical needs, and even as Ginger was brought to tears expressing to me over coffee her fears and frustrations regarding some of these needs, she didn't hesitate to say that their family would be open to another special-needs adoption. They are willing to fill their family with all the pieces it needs to create a beautiful completion. Each of their children with each of their unique needs and gifts fills up an empty space within their family.

"That is our purpose, where we are called," Ginger told me.

We all belong. We all bring an extraordinarily unique beauty with us as we work together and give the world what we have to offer—our gifts, our talents, our time, our resources, our kindness and appreciation, our relationships, our purpose, and our calling. The people we gather together in our lives help to complete us, and we are essential to the lives of people who love us as well.

The world needs you and only one of you to create an incredible impact with your colors and shapes. The world needs you and only one of you to bring a different beautiful into this magnificent puzzle.

# CHAPTER 18

## Turning Our Eyes from the Mirror to Others' Hearts

"So they need help," my best friend Kristin said to me one morning as our kids ran around her basement. "And I think it would be really great if we could get everyone together to hold a drive."

She had explained that a local nonprofit that serves the poor of our community—which her grandfather had been instrumental in helping to run before his death—had seen such an increase in need that they could now only afford to provide food items to their clients and not personal care items, like soap and toilet paper. With her family's continued involvement in this organization, they had seen what a need there was for toilet paper, a basic necessity but often an extra expense that simply couldn't be covered.

This single conversation sparked action within our group of friends.

A date was set, a venue was booked, and Facebook invitations were sent out. We coordinated food and drinks, a fifty-fifty raffle, signs, media coverage, and a large flatbed truck on which to stack rolls of toilet paper. And we were graced with the most beautiful June weather as our friends, family, and complete strangers brought pack after pack of toilet paper to this event we dubbed "TP the Town."

Our community stepped up to purchase this basic need that we throw into our shopping carts when we run out without a second thought but that many people with low income struggle to pay for. With our TP the Town drive, my friends collected more than five thousand rolls of toilet paper and a couple thousand dollars of cash for this non-profit that aids our community's poor.

Within the year following that first toilet paper drive, God continued to move our hearts to serve.

My friends and I began to keep our eyes and our hearts open to many other opportunities to help where we felt God calling us. We collected personal care items for the children at a low-income after-school program, and we purchased small toys and art supplies to fill stockings for impoverished children at another program. We made dinner for the women at a local homeless shelter one winter evening, where we piled food on plate after plate and then sat down to chat with these fellow moms.

We even put together dozens of bags of birthday supplies so that children at the homeless shelter could have birthday parties, thanks largely in part to a community grant that my friend Emily secured to provide us with the financial resources to do that.

Then, two years after our first toilet paper drive—taking

a year off when six babies were born within our group!—we held a second TP the Town event that garnered tremendous support from our community and topped our collection at more than ten thousand rolls of toilet paper.

I witnessed over and over a group of busy moms making time again and again to step forward and take action to make a difference within our community. Not only was I humbled by (and admittedly proud of) our efforts, but I began to notice a very interesting trend that evolved.

Most conversations about our appearances have all but faded away.

As we began to talk about our faith and our purpose and about where God was calling us to help and about what action steps needed to be taken for the betterment of our community, there were no more comments about having a bad hair day. There were no more texts about "WHAT ARE YOU WEARING OUT TO DINNER TONIGHT?" There were no more lamentations about feeling fat or being saggy after having three kids.

We had become more concerned with others than with ourselves; we were too busy looking outward to look in the mirror.

I've noticed that the more we look in the mirror, the more we begin to examine ourselves—and criticize ourselves. And as we spend that time on ourselves, as we stare harder at the mirror, we lose sight of those around us.

The night that my friends and I gathered at the women's shelter with our carefully planned and prepared dinner, we had just passed around dessert when we realized one of us had gone missing. We finally noticed Emily sitting among the women at one of the large picnic-style tables, writing down her recipe for the delicious dessert she had made that night—saltine crackers covered with melted butter and brown sugar with chocolate melted on top. It was so tasty that the women at the shelter were asking for seconds and thirds.

"Thank you, these were so good." One of the women smiled gratefully as Emily passed her the piece of paper.

Emily had taken the initiative to connect. She didn't let the fact that she has never been homeless stop her from building a bridge and looking into the hearts of those staying at the shelter as simply fellow mothers and women. And with that simple gesture, she paved the way for the rest of our group to join the women and talk about their families and their lives.

Without truly listening, our perceptions are just that—perceptions. We perceive, assume, and make judgments without really trying to understand. But when we take the time to listen to another person's story, we can see beyond what that person looks like on the outside and begin to understand what he or she is made of on the inside.

Life becomes about the feelings and needs of others instead of ourselves.

Author Mandy Hale writes in her book: "Nothing is more beautiful than someone who goes out of her way to make life beautiful for others."[19]

It makes me wonder about the dozens of self-esteem programs that are now permeating our schools and communities. It makes me wonder if, instead of spending week after week trying to build up the sense of self-worth in each of these participating children—and especially girls—with various games and programs and speakers, maybe we should set down the mirror. Could we be focusing so much on self-acceptance, self-worth, self-esteem, self-confidence that our kids then only think about how me, myself, and *I* feel?

Have we inadvertently created generations with raging self-centeredness? Have we pushed aside humility in favor of esteeming oneself? Are we giving our kids too many mirrors instead of blinders?

Perhaps, instead, the most effective way to feel better about ourselves is to do something for someone else. Sometimes I think showing kindness to someone else or making someone's life just a little bit better has the power to build up your sense of self-worth more than any self-help program or book or seminar ever could.

In his book *A Million Miles in a Thousand Years*, Donald

19. Mandy Hale, *The Single Woman: Life, Love, and a Dash of Sass* (Nashville: Thomas Nelson, 2013), 160.

Miller writes about his friend Jason's family who was experiencing problems with his teenage daughter, who was experimenting with drugs and dating a guy who smelled like smoke and was indifferent toward everyone around him. No amount of yelling or grounding or any other measure was helping the situation, and it was getting worse.

But then Donald commented that Jason's daughter was living a terrible story, that she wasn't looking outward with her life and living with purpose to make a difference to others.

When Donald ran into Jason a few months later, he couldn't believe how much better the family was doing. What had changed? Jason shared that they had begun to live a better story together, taking risks to work toward common goals that would make a bigger and more positive impact on the world.

Without consulting any of the other members of his family, one day Jason had decided to pledge to help raise $25,000 to build an orphanage in Mexico—money that the family certainly didn't have lying around, but nonetheless, he explained to his wife that "they weren't taking risks and weren't helping anybody and how their daughter was losing interest."

Within days, his wife told him she was proud of him— something she hadn't said in a long time—and his daughter began planning a trip to Mexico to become more invested in this project and share with others about it and fundraise for the orphanage.

Oh, and his daughter broke up with her boyfriend.

"No girl who plays the role of a hero dates a guy who uses her," Jason told Don. "She knows who she is. She just forgot for a little while."[20]

When we choose to turn away from the mirror and invest in the lives of others, that offers us not only a tremendous opportunity to change the world for the better, to live out Jesus' call for our lives, but also the capability of building ourselves up far more than any kind of beauty regime or self-help program could.

---

20. Donald Miller, *A Million Miles in a Thousand Years* (Nashville: Thomas Nelson, 2009), 54.

# CHAPTER 19

## Using Our Differences as Gifts for the World

There were two weeks left before Christmas.

Our family battled the thick traffic in front of the strip mall where Target was located, and Evan pulled up in front of the door so I could quickly jump out.

There wasn't a cart left to grab at the entrance, and the lines at the cashier's counters wound around with shopping carts full of toys and clothes that would soon be wrapped in candy cane wrapping paper and set under a brightly decorated fir tree.

I didn't need a cart, and the line didn't bother me. As I walked over to the coffee café at the front of the store, I slowly scanned the tables before turning back toward the doors.

I didn't find what I came for. . .but it wasn't a toy or a purse or a pair of shoes. It was a person.

The first time I saw him, weeks prior, I knew who he was.

When Brenna was around six months old, the local newspaper wrote a large story about her and our family on the cover of the paper; it ran on Father's Day. A woman contacted the reporter soon after to tell her that she had met a homeless man "with the same condition."

Frankly, we were a bit skeptical. We knew that an older man wouldn't have the exact type of Brenna's condition because the oldest living person with it was twenty-nine at the time, and in England.

And we were overwhelmed. Just six months in, we were still barely keeping our heads above water when it came to caring for Brenna's skin. That summer when she was a baby was, no doubt, one of the most difficult periods of our lives.

Brenna was hospitalized several times for dehydration, she was treated for infections, and she stopped eating well. We agonized over what to do about her weight loss and often-occurring bouts with dehydration because she wasn't drinking her bottles like she had been—and nothing seemed to help.

Just six weeks after that article ran, Brenna was hospitalized for a week and underwent a surgery to have a g-tube placed in her stomach.

Our high hopes for that feeding tube gave way in actuality to lots of trials that included skin complications and constant vomiting. It was a desperate time for us, and Brenna was so sick that her precious little eight-month-old face didn't smile for a whole month. A whole *month*.

Suffice it to say that when the newspaper reporter showed me this stranger's message about a homeless man with the "same condition," I simply told her to thank the woman.

And I forgot about it.

Until I saw him two and a half years later.

I actually saw him twice before I decided to say hello. I was browsing the toy department of Target with Brenna while Connor was at school (sometimes I let my kids look at the toys without picking one out. I'm a really nice mom like that).

He walked by me, and I spoke up. "Excuse me. Do you have ichthyosis?"

I knew immediately he did when I first saw him because I recognized it in his eyes, which were pulled tightly open, revealing bright red and irritated upper and lower lids areas. His skin was patchy and thick and looked dirty, though I knew most of that unclean appearance was probably because of the condition, not from actual dirtiness.

He stopped, startled, and said yes. He looked at Brenna as I told him, "So does my daughter."

"Were you the ones in the paper?" he asked. He remembered.

We stood in that aisle among dolls and My Little Pony toys and talked for a half hour. His name was Michael, and he shared pieces of his story with me. He was sixty years old and had been homeless for a couple different periods in the last four years. Although I could tell he wanted to be the one to be a source of information and encouragement for us, he was so uneducated about his own skin condition that he asked me, "Do you know why I can't sweat? Do I not have sweat glands, or is the skin too thick?" (I informed him that I had recently learned that for people with ichthyosis, the skin is too thick and won't allow sweat to emerge on the surface.)

Sixty years ago was a different world for this condition, and he told me he hadn't seen a dermatologist in many years. He wanted to but was afraid of getting stuck with a bill he couldn't pay if his state-funded medical care didn't cover something.

After a half hour, Brenna was asking, quite determinedly, to go, so I reluctantly told Michael good-bye but that I would try to find him again.

I'm ashamed to say that was the first time in my entire life that I talked with someone who is homeless. And with that short conversation, something inside my heart opened up. God placed that man in my life at a time when I would have normally been starting to stress out about Christmas shopping, holiday traditions, and cooking for Christmas gatherings—the kinds of things that we focus on instead of the fact that there are people, our brothers and sisters, huddled in alleys with nothing. *Nothing*.

Or in Michael's case, sleeping in a cardboard Dumpster, wrapped up in the cardboard with the lid shut to protect him from the cold and rain.

That day, the face of the homeless came into clear view. The face of Jesus sharpened into focus. All because my daughter was born with this severe skin disorder.

I put together a little care package for Michael after our initial meeting with some skin care products and gift cards to local restaurants. And one entire Saturday morning following that day, our family searched for him in the area where we knew he stayed. We fought the holiday crowds to dart into stores and look around for him, and we drove behind closed restaurants. We saw makeshift homes of cardboard set up in nooks against abandoned buildings to provide as much shelter as possible from the bitter cold December winds, and my heart ached for the men and women who lived with that kind of survival and that kind of lack.

We didn't find him that day, and we didn't find him with another couple of tries.

On December 19, I walked into Target as it was opening, and I saw him. It was, fittingly, Brenna's third birthday.

We had breakfast in the café with Michael that morning. He confided to me that he was worried about Christmas Day because the stores he frequented every day for protection from the weather would be closed.

After I shared about Michael's predicament with our family and friends, everyone began looking into a way to get Michael off the street for Christmas, and Christmas Eve brought a flurry of texts concerned about this one man and his welfare. My dad finally found him on the afternoon of Christmas Eve, and we were able to book a hotel room for him.

My parents stepped in that winter to buy a hotel room for him on several more occasions as our central Illinois temperatures dropped like crazy. And as summer approached, we then began to worry about Michael's skin in the heat.

Because of our experiences with raising Brenna and caring for her skin, we had a unique vantage point of knowing what many of Michael's needs are. Brenna's pediatric dermatologist helped us set up an appointment with an adult dermatologist for Michael—his first in years—and we have given him some of our favorite skin care products to try.

And we knew he needed, desperately, to get off the streets, as he was at a very increased risk of infection and of overheating as the hot summer months approached.

My family now has a much better understanding about why the homeless stay homeless. Because receiving benefits like food stamps and applying for low-income housing is an absolute mess of bureaucracy and paperwork and forms and needing to obtain items like birth certificates. And in some cases, even needing an *address*.

But our God is bigger.

My mom is a social worker. And we have a good family friend who worked at the social security administration office and helped us immensely in navigating the regulations and programs and benefits and applications.

And in July, six months after he walked into our lives in the toy aisle in Target, Michael walked through the door of his new apartment.

God doesn't mean for us to discern who is worthy of our compassion and love. He just tells us to care for the oppressed. He tells us to serve "the least of these."

God bestows incredible gifts on each of us, unique pieces of ourselves that we are meant to share with the world to reveal God's beauty in the world. Our gifts and talents, our time and resources are to be used to serve. And because of each of our varying life experiences and the way God has moved in our hearts, our differences can be tremendous gifts in changing the lives of those around us. Using and sharing our differences might change someone's circumstances, change someone's future, or change someone's heart toward Jesus. Or hopefully, all three.

Our differences help to designate our purpose in this life.

God uses every aspect of us, including adversity, difference, and even failure, to reach us and to reach others. We are who He designed us to be, and He is using our incredible uniqueness to change hearts toward Him and to work for the good of His plans.

I'm guessing that when we get to heaven, God won't want to talk about our opinions or even our beliefs quite as much as He'll want to talk about how we served our brothers and sisters. Not what we said or thought while we lived but what we *did*—how we used the differences that He gifted us with in order to serve and help and build up others.

Even when our differences feel isolating, God is connecting. Even when we are struggling, God is redeeming.

Such as the man I met who grew up without his father, a father who walked out on the family when he was very young, who now runs a mentoring program for young boys being raised by single mothers.

Or the woman I know with visual differences who hosts events for tween girls to affirm to them how much the Lord values them, no matter what they look like.

Or the woman who is biracial and is now working at a struggling school district, bridging the students with a variety of backgrounds and colors.

The things that made these people feel very different from those around them are now the gifts they are sharing to better the world.

And because of Brenna's skin disorder, there is one less homeless person on the street.

# CHAPTER 20

## Laundry Stains

*I* slipped my heels on as I rattled off care instructions to my parents, who would be watching Brenna for the rest of the evening while Evan, Connor, and I attended a wedding reception.

With a 6:00 p.m. wedding, the reception ran well past her bedtime (Connor's, too, but his attendance was more important as a ring bearer!), so Brenna was freshly covered in Aquaphor and pajamas while I donned a deep turquoise strapless dress for my night out celebrating.

Perhaps as a result of so many doctors' visits and hospitalizations during her first year of life, Brenna had developed stranger anxiety very early on and was very wary of anyone who, well, wasn't me.

That night, my eighteen-month-old began to wail and reach for me, so without thinking, I picked her up and set her on my hip. I carried her around while I pointed out the rest of the instructions—how much formula to put into Brenna's feeding pump and how to program the pump, what time to feed her, and more—to my parents before I turned my upset girl over to her grandparents.

I turned to go and saw my mom's face, a mix of dismay and sympathy.

There on my side, on my colorful blue dress, a deep, oily stain had settled in.

Once upon a time, I would have cried at that stain.

I really wanted to wear that turquoise dress. We had several weddings that summer, and I was trying to rotate my small assortment of formalwear for each event. I had styled my hair and chosen my makeup, jewelry, and shoes to complement that dress.

I debated if anyone would notice the dark spot on my side. After an examination in the mirror, I realized it was pretty obvious, and a little weird to go to a fancy wedding with a stained dress.

So I changed. I grabbed my purse and quickly headed out the door, smiling as I closed it behind me.

I changed my dress. . .but I felt my insides also changing that night. I began to understand that evening that stains have the power to ruin only when we let them.

Because Brenna's skin doesn't retain moisture, it dries out extremely fast. The remedy for this is to use a cream or emollient on a frequent basis. Aquaphor, made by a company called Beiersdorf, is the lotion of choice for many families who are affected by skin conditions because its properties and effectiveness are ideal compared to other lotions on the market. We have tried several at varying thickness and greasiness, but we always come back to Aquaphor as our favorite.

A thin streak of Aquaphor on my own skin at night lasts until I wash it off in the morning; Brenna's skin dries out in a matter of a couple of hours, with no noticeable lotion residue and thin flakes that begin to peel off her body.

Four or five times each day, we swipe a large dollop of Aquaphor from the largest jars the company makes and spread it out over Brenna's entire body, using vinyl medical gloves so we contain the Aquaphor and so we don't spread unnecessary germs between our skin and Brenna's.

This ongoing routine keeps Brenna's skin moisturized and supple enough to move. Without regular lotion, her skin would dry out and crack, becoming extremely painful and dehydrated.

What makes Aquaphor so effective for dry skin also makes it very effective elsewhere. Like walls. And furniture. And clothing.

We also have to be careful with bleach. Because Brenna's skin lacks the typical barrier to protect her body from outside germs, we will add a small amount of bleach to her bath every few days—especially days where she comes in contact with a lot of people when risk of germs is high.

It's enough bleach to kill unwanted bacteria, but it doesn't burn—similar to a swimming pool's chlorine content.

When Brenna was a few months old, I stood up from the bathtub with her wrapped cozily in her towel, and Evan gestured to my brand-new sweatpants. "You got some bleach on the back."

Tears welled in my eyes.

Ruined. They were ruined. Just like a couple of T-shirts, a pair of jeans, and another top had already been ruined.

Clothing has never been a priority in my life; my friends will assure you that I am no fashionista. But in the beginning of Brenna's life, as we grappled with our new lifestyle of skin care and health care, the little things built up in my head as big things. Things like not being able to dress my daughter in clothing with velvet or lace or knowing that her clothes would be ruined after a couple times of wear. And things like having to "save" certain outfits of my own for times when I wasn't caring for Brenna.

These little issues just seemed like one more thing to have to think about in the midst of simply worrying about keeping her alive and healthy. And occasionally, I struggled with coming to terms with the effects Brenna's skin care routine was having on so many aspects of our lives, even unimportant things like our clothes.

I do what I can to save my clothing from the grease. But I have always, and will always, choose Brenna's cuddles over protecting my clothes. And so, occasionally a stain will slip through unnoticed, warmed into permanence by the dryer.

The first time I washed a load of Brenna's clothing in our washing machine, I stood in shock when I opened the lid of the completed cycle.

Chunks of thick grease coated the sides of our washer, needing to be scrubbed off with Dawn dish soap over and over with each load. Elbow grease took on a very literal meaning as I developed a daily laundry routine that involved both washing clothes and then washing the washing machine.

When Brenna was two and a half years old, we moved to a new home that afforded us the space to have two washing machines—one for her Aquaphor-laden clothes, and one for the rest of us.

However, after a few months of usage, it became clear that this new washing model was quite inferior to our previous home's old model. While the old model would spin the Aquaphor to the top, where I could clean it off after each load, the new machine would spin it to an outer, hidden basin—where it would build up and continue to keep her clothes greasy.

It got to the point where my hands would have a thin layer of grease after folding Brenna's clothes. But we had to take apart the entire washer just to clean out the Aquaphor.

So we did what anyone would do: we knocked on the

door of our old home—which in that time, had already been sold to someone other than the person who bought it from us—and asked to buy our clunky ten-year-old washing machine back.

And without hesitation, the new owners said yes. God bless them.

I brought my old friend home and threw in some of Brenna's grease-soaked shirts that I was about to toss in the garbage because I thought they were as good as goners.

After that first load, the top of my beloved workhorse of a washing machine was caked in chunks of Aquaphor once again—and Brenna's shirts were like new again.

They just needed a little more elbow grease than we had previously had. (Pardon the pun.)

These days, I carefully choose my wardrobe, mostly because I don't like to be wasteful or extravagant. If I know my daily wardrobe is going to be subjected to battles with grease, I don't need to put up extra effort to fight back when I could be spending my energy—and money—elsewhere. Six-dollar shirts on sale at Target—striped cotton ones, to be specific—have become a wardrobe staple for me.

And those stains on the sides of my shirts where I hold my daughter or the markings on my jeans where she sits no longer bother me one bit. Sometimes I am able to remove the stains...but other times, I can be found chucking a shirt into the trash after a couple of seasons of intense

Aquaphor exposure. More often than not, I am thankful for what those shirts gave me—day after day of not worrying about what stains might be incurring from cuddling, holding, carrying, and rocking with my child.

In the early days, I used to be prone to change more often before going out into public. I wondered what others would think about the grease streaks on my shirts. But now I see those streaks as part of my motherhood story. Now I leave my stained shirts on for Target runs.

Maybe stains aren't tainting but are telling. Maybe instead, stains stand for intense beauty, helping to tell our incredible stories in all kinds of ways. What first seems "broken" can be redeemed to an incredible story in the name of our Lord.

We give stains too much power. Too often, we let them dictate ruin on whatever they touch.

But stains have an intense beauty if we look hard enough. It's the same for wrinkles and other marks on our clothes, our bodies, or our hearts. These things often represent tenacity, character, pure love. When something is stained or worn, it is usually because it has been well loved or very useful.

I worked and worked on that turquoise dress I wore the night of the wedding with its side stain of Aquaphor where my daughter sat on my hip. I tried spray after spray of stain remover. However, I must have waited too long, or maybe the fabric just wasn't conducive to greasiness. The stain stuck.

But that dress hangs in my closet still, and I smile at it thinking about that night and recalling how much my heart has changed since and because of that stain.

Sometimes, stains just need a little extra effort to become fresh and clean again, like with the first load run in our old washing machine. But then again, some stains are worth appreciating simply for what they mean in our lives.

# CHAPTER 21

## When Faith Means Trusting and Waiting

In the middle of the kind of life that many people dream of, my friend Megan felt a kind of invitation from the Lord that challenged everything she had known up until that point. Megan had a wonderful husband, two healthy and thriving children, life in the suburbs in Colorado with friendships and church. . .but she and her husband simply couldn't ignore whispers from God that plucked them from this life and expanded their family from across the world in Ethiopia.

As they followed this invitation, Megan found that it is far easier to declare "Lord, send me" than to truly consider what may come along with that bold statement, especially when God wanted to send her into so much unknown.

Sometimes we tend to think of adoption stories in terms of the real work leading up to the adoption—paperwork, waiting, caseworker visits, court documents, and more—and the happily-ever-after that begins the minute the child is placed into his or her waiting family's arms. The fairy tales of children added to their new families often end on the big screen with the homecoming. But as Megan discovered, this new life and new family dynamic can be a drastic change for all involved and can bring intense emotional struggles.

Megan's two children adopted from Ethiopia were five and nearly eight years old and spoke hardly a word of English when they moved to Colorado. The first year especially was extremely hard as they all fought to find their footing as part of this new family that had been created with the adoptions.

Megan struggled to understand how something she and her husband, Scott, felt so divinely led to do was causing this kind of turmoil within their lives. To Megan and Scott, adopting felt like God's provision for their new children, but to their adopted children, "it felt like they had been kidnapped from their country," Megan said.

"I believe that adoption is a way to connect to the heart of God and a way to love God's people, but we have to remember that it also comes from a very broken place," Megan told me. "We realized that it was no longer just a choice Scott and I had made for ourselves—this decision impacted the future of four children. Even when you choose to follow God's call, sometimes that has a direct impact on someone else, especially children who have no say in the matter, and it can feel very heavy."[21]

But even in this heaviness, Megan found God showing up. Even on the very difficult days, Megan and Scott were

---

21. Megan Nilsen (author of *A Beautiful Exchange*) in discussion with the author, October 2015.

able to see, in their children, the kingdom of God in full Technicolor beauty, even in the middle of intense brokenness and hurt.

I really don't like the phrase "God only gives us what we can handle," but it's one that people return to again and again to explain hardships or to provide comfort. While meant to offer encouragement, I'm not sure we wouldn't really even need God if we truly could "handle it" ourselves.

I think life is full of triumphs and challenges, good and bad, ups and downs, and I think everyone reacts to situations and experiences differently based on a huge variety of circumstances.

I believe that life, with all its suffering and brokenness, hands us so much more than we could ever handle. But in those times of great need is where we are most likely to turn to God to hold us up, to walk next to us, to fill us up.

This phrase is derived from 1 Corinthians 10:13, which says: "God is faithful; he will not let you to be tempted beyond what you can bear. But when you are tempted, he will also provide a way out so that you can endure it."

God promises we will be able to "bear" anything because of Him.

What I believe God actually gives us is the opportunity to rely on Him in every situation we encounter, in every emotion we feel, and in every decision we make.

God has promised to be there for us, always—in times

we may not understand and in ways we may not understand, but He is there. And it's not always easy for us to relinquish this control. We try to plan, we try to control, and we try to understand why.

But sometimes we just need to rely on God and to wait.

There will always be parts of our lives that confront our trust and patience with God. Waiting doesn't mean testing God, asking Him to prove Himself. Waiting doesn't mean forgetting about God until He reaches out to us.

Sometimes waiting means that God is working in us and preparing us even when to us that waiting can feel desperate and frustrating.

"Many times we feel like giving up because we forget how much God really loves us. When negative emotions overtake our minds and hearts, we lose focus on the love of God," Rachel Wojo writes in her book *One More Step*. "Hope can be placed anywhere we choose, but the place we choose makes all the difference. When we place our hope in Christ, we are delivered."[22]

In order to wait and to hope, we must first trust. We need to trust that God loves us *no matter what*, and even though we may not understand everything in this world, our lives are part of a grand plan in which He is sharing Himself and His beautiful, perfect love through us.

Suffering is one of those pieces of life that is nearly

---

22. Rachel Wojo, *One More Step* (Colorado Springs: WaterBrook, 2015), 16, 30–31.

impossible to comprehend. Why must people suffer? Why must people, and especially children, experience pain and destruction and fear and grief?

So much going on in our world today is because of the choices humankind has made over time—choosing to fight and to harm. And these choices have come from the free will first given to Adam and Eve. But devastations like natural disasters or disease? Couldn't God just swoop in and save us all from every part of suffering?

Couldn't God just make Brenna's skin better? Couldn't God just make her healthy?

I think the more we try to understand, the less we actually comprehend.

"'For my thoughts are not your thoughts, neither are your ways my ways,'" declares the Lord in Isaiah 55:8. Nowhere in the Bible did God say He would make life easier for us for the sake of an easy and carefree life. In fact, in many stories of the Bible, He intentionally allowed suffering in order to reveal Himself to people.

I'm not sure the opposite of suffering is well-being. I think it is only within and because of suffering that we can find true and lasting peace. Accepting life's difficulties as part of humanity offers us a choice: to do life and all its challenges with God or without Him.

When someone asks me why God "let this happen" to Brenna, I could respond a million different ways, with arguments and scripture, or even agree with them, that aren't life and God so unfair?

But truly, the answer is that I don't know. And I'm at peace with not knowing, because I put my faith and my trust in Him every day.

That control is unbelievably hard to relinquish sometimes.

This is hard when my beloved daughter is lying on a hospital bed, and I'm gently gripping her tiny hand and holding down her thrashing legs while the medical team tries—often failing—to find a vein in her arm, and she's crying in pain and screaming for it to be "all done."

This is hard when she's anxiously clinging to me, asking in fear what the nurse is "going to do to me" because she has learned people wearing scrubs often cause major discomfort.

This is hard when she's uncontrollably scratching herself in the middle of the night, unable to get comfortable and succumb to sleep because her skin is so itchy.

This is hard when she's cringing and crying at the onset of a skin infection, as her skin feels painful and raw all over her body.

It is in moments like this that I don't want to blindly trust. I just want my daughter to be better, to be healed, and to not have to experience this kind of pain, and worse.

But I have found that this kind of suffering can also

produce an unabridged joy, an immense appreciation for the simplest of moments that give us peace in our smallness and love of the goodness of life. Because of trials, the good in life becomes better.

"Consider it pure joy, my brothers and sisters," James tells us in James 1:2–4, "whenever you face trials of many kinds, because you know that the testing of your faith produces perseverance. Let perseverance finish its work so that you may be mature and complete, not lacking anything."

And because of and within this kind of suffering, these trials, we can come to know God, to form the deepest kind of relationship with Him.

He doesn't necessarily stop all the suffering in the world, just as He didn't stop Jesus' suffering. But instead He meets us in our suffering and in our hardships, and He gives us Himself and everything that comes with that— unconditional love and healing and forgiveness. And this is made possible because of Jesus' ultimate sacrifice of His life for us, so that we may live forever in God's amazing love.

God fills where we lack. God holds tight when we are stretching too far. God heals and makes whole, and we can only know this incredible healing and wholeheartedness as we rise up from our despair and suffering.

"The Lord is a God of justice," says Isaiah 30:18. "He will rise up to show you compassion. . . . Blessed are all who wait for him!"

So does God give us what we can handle? It feels like the answer may be absolutely not.

But He gives us so much more and so much better—He has given us Jesus, and He has offered His perfect love to us. And it is, perhaps, the times we are most hurting that we can recognize this and say, "Yes, we accept. We need You, Lord, and we want You. Even when we don't understand."

As she battled with a diagnosis of breast cancer at just thirty-six years old, mother of four Kara Tippetts found the peace of God even in the midst of her inconceivable sickness and suffering. Kara, who passed away in 2015, spoke incredible truth when she said, "Suffering isn't a mistake and isn't the absence of God's goodness, because He's present in pain."[23]

Faith comes not from understanding but from trusting. . .trusting in His ways even when they are not at all our ways.

I know there were times in my friend Megan's adoption journey where she wanted to question if this had been the right decision. The duality of motherhood has brought a battle for control within her in many situations, leaving her with the choice of whether to exercise all parental control and authority or whether to relinquish that need for control to follow Jesus —exchanging "my need to control

23. Kara Tippetts, *Kara Tippetts Documentary Trailer*, video, February 22, 2015.

for His Spirit of love," she writes in her book, *A Beautiful Exchange*.[24]

Even in her days of despair, she waited for God. Even when it was extremely hard, she trusted God.

And God found Megan in her struggles and revealed Himself in a much bigger way within this new family He had brought together.

"Having our two adopted kids helps us connect with others in ways we never could have before," Megan said she has realized. "This melding of souls actually ushers us into new and deeper places of connection simply because we are blending people from different places, contexts, and experiences. Our transracial family opens doors to the Kingdom we may not have walked through previously."[25]

Emotionally, physically, mentally, financially—when we have more than we can handle, we have our trust in God. And He meets us in our hardship, carries us through, and reveals the beauty of His kingdom.

24. Megan Nilsen, *A Beautiful Exchange* (Maitland, FL: Xulon, 2015), 125.
25. Megan Nilsen (author of *A Beautiful Exchange*) in discussion with the author, October 2015.

# CHAPTER 22

## Only as Limiting as We Make It

Since she doesn't have the ability to sweat, heat can be dangerous for Brenna, which means that summers have a new meaning for our family. The kind of winters that people in the Midwest complain about—poor weather, being cooped up inside—are also true for our family in summer. Summer doesn't offer us easy days at the pool or outdoor day camps or even going to the park without weather concerns.

No matter the time of year now, if we receive an invitation in the mail to an outdoor event, my stomach tightens a bit. *What will the weather be like?*

When Connor was four years old, we registered him for fall soccer, and his first game neared with a prediction of a balmy ninety-degree Saturday morning.

The evening before, we prepared Brenna's cooling vest for the occasion—two big cold packs that are created to remain at fifty-five degrees for two hours that are inserted into a little vest and draped over the shoulders to keep the body's core temperature cooled off during a hot day.

That morning, as the pack of cleated kids haphazardly chased the soccer ball—or chased dragonflies, depending on the kid—Evan and I sat vigilantly with Brenna packed up in her cooling vest, taking turns holding a spray fan to her face.

All the other little siblings dashed around the sidelines of the soccer field, sweat dripping down their necks and foreheads, their parents hardly giving them a second glance. And there was no doubt that it was much more consuming and stressful to have to worry about keeping our daughter's temperature stable, but when the whistle blew for that game to end, we wanted to high-five.

We did it.

We took on our first intolerably hot day without Brenna overheating, without letting the fear of the heat override attending Connor's game as a family.

When Brenna was first born, realization after realization hit as we considered the limits of this severe skin disorder. We are a water-loving family, and we have spent vacations and weekends each summer swimming and boating on the lake. We are active and social, and we love sports.

As we thought about Brenna's future, it seemed impossible to imagine her playing softball in the hot summer heat. It seemed impossible to think about boating and swimming as a family with the fear of bacteria in the lake. It seemed impossible to picture us building snowmen and sledding down fluffy white hills in the winter.

Finally, one day, I realized I wasn't putting forth the

effort to include Brenna in activities or projects that the kids around us were participating in, simply because it might be very difficult for her, or because she wasn't mobile yet and would need a lot of extra help.

Yet, I also knew she would need to be held to the same standards as other children, including her brother—regarding participation in events and activities, regarding discipline and behavior, and everything else in life—in order to be empowered.

If we placed unnecessary limits on her, she would only continue to do the same herself as she grew older. If we placed unnecessary limits on her, we would be showing her a kind of pity.

Finally, when we were at a school carnival one fall, I realized that even though I might need to assist her more, she should be able to take part in what all the other kids were doing. It was there that I held her close to the ring toss and helped her "toss" the rings, and I helped her push the ball toward the bowling pins. And she loved every second of those games.

She may need extra accommodations or help to complete a task or art project, but that is not unique to only her. We all need extra help when it comes to things we may not have mastered yet.

Evan and I have pushed ourselves outside of our comfort zone again and again, with Brenna's first boat ride, her first vacation to a water park, and her first time playing in the snow. And with each experience, we have grown more confident as her parents, and we have witnessed her confidence grow.

"You can't do that" is a phrase we try to suppress. If anyone is going to decide Brenna can't do something, we want it to be Brenna.

Despite all its limitations—from physical and motor issues to concerns about temperature and germs—ultimately, we have found that Brenna's condition is only as limiting as we let it be. And we want to model to her that she can do anything and be anything she wants, regardless of her skin. We don't want fear to hold us back from enjoying life.

So many pieces of our lives can be limited solely by the limitations we place on ourselves. We let our fears and our doubts restrict what we feel capable of completing or accomplishing or even simply trying.

In many cases with Brenna, we've simply had to adjust a bit, to get creative with how we're able to do what we want to do. We've set our own paths without putting limits on what we can do. And this is true for so many people— we simply may need to make some adjustments depending on where we are in life.

I was in fifth grade when I met a man named Roger Crawford. And I was nervous about shaking his hand.

Roger was born with only two fingers on one hand and a thumb on the other hand. One of his feet has three toes, and the other leg was so underdeveloped, it was amputated below his knee.

In my little ten-year-old mind, I couldn't conceive how it would be to shake a hand with fewer than five fingers, and I felt awkward.

To this day, I don't even remember the actual handshake.

What I remember is how I immediately felt at ease and in awe of him. Roger is such a dynamic personality that I could have listened to him talk all day. And he made me feel interesting as he asked me questions about my sports teams.

When I picture Roger Crawford now as an adult, all I can see is his bright smile. I can't tell you exactly how his hands and legs look or don't look, but I can always see his warm smile that drew me into our conversation.

Meeting Roger was my first introduction to pushing beyond personal limitations.

From the beginning of his life, Roger's parents pushed him toward excellence. Instead of growing up accepting that his future would likely not include sports because of his limb abnormalities, he trained and challenged himself to pursue his dreams of playing tennis.

Participating in college athletics is a feat enough in

itself, but it's especially impressive when you're missing most of your fingers on both hands and part of your leg.

Roger adapted to his limited hand capabilities by holding his tennis racket in the middle opening instead of the handle, and he learned to move quickly on his feet with a prosthetic.

He ended up becoming the first person with a physical challenge affecting two or more limbs to play NCAA Division I athletics. Eventually, he was inducted as a Hall of Fame Division I Athlete. *Sports Illustrated* recognized Roger as "one of the most accomplished physically challenged athletes in the world," and in 2013 he was selected as the winner of the ITA Achievement Award, presented by the International Tennis Hall of Fame and the highest honor bestowed by the Intercollegiate Tennis Association.

What Roger took away from his extraordinary accomplishments is that we can all learn to "redefine the possible."

"I learned," he said, "that I wasn't going to be the fastest or the most powerful, but if I could hit the ball over the net one more time than my opponent, then I'd win the point.

"I grew up with the belief that everyone has challenges— some you can see and some you can't."

Years after meeting him for the first time, I asked Roger about limitations and obstacles.

For many young people with disabilities and even able-bodied children, sometimes their parents are their greatest limitation. Often, this comes from fear; we don't want child to be hurt, or we might have certain perceptions of what our children are capable of.

But it's so important to allow our children to fulfill their potential. To allow them to amaze us with their abilities, because we really don't know what they can accomplish until we give them those opportunities to excel.

The greatest gift his parents gave him, Roger said, is the opportunity to attempt and succeed. . .or fail.

"What I realized when I was young is that yes, I had some limitations, but I also had some gifts— and it was about what I wanted to focus on," he said.[26]

Not only do we set limits on ourselves and our children, but so often we set limits on God, too.

But there is a redefined beauty found in doing things beyond what is comfortable or beyond what we see by playing into society's standards of what is expected—or not expected.

We are God's *masterpieces*. He created us in His image, and He celebrates over each of us and what we are capable of doing, through Him.

We are fearfully and wonderfully made in His image, and we are strengthened by Him as we seek out and fulfill our purpose and live out our passions. Sometimes, we ask

---

26. Roger Crawford (author of *Think Again!* and National Speakers Association Hall of Fame member) in discussion with the author, October 2015.

for or expect very limited things from our Lord, instead of allowing Him to work through us to accomplish the amazing, the unbelievable, even the impossible.

When Roger Crawford went to school each year, his parents encouraged him to wear shorts and short-sleeved shirts, so that all his classmates could see his physical differences immediately—and "then move on."

> *I know a lot of other parents thought that was really harsh of them, but they wanted me to confront it from the very beginning. And I know that took a kind of courage for them, as parents, but they were right. It made me realize that you've got to give kids a chance to succeed and if you're going to do that, there are going to be times where they are pushed out of their comfort zones. . . . And that's true for any child.[27]*

Roger and his parents found a redefined beauty and accomplishment outside of the comfortable.

Evan and I decided in the very beginning of Brenna's life that we did not want to be the ones to tell her that she couldn't do something if she wanted to try it.

Of course, we take precautions to keep our daughter healthy, but we strive every day not to be overcautious. We get together with friends usually a couple times a week,

---

27. Crawford, discussion with the author, October 2015.

and I love that Brenna has a whole horde of her own friends now. . .kids she has grown up with and who don't even notice her skin and probably never will, because it is their normal now. We go to the park, to the museum, to the library, to restaurants, on vacations. In her first three years of life, Brenna had already traveled to eleven states!

Brenna is able to do *so much more* than she can't do. And we are able to do, as a family, so much more than I ever thought we would after learning of her diagnosis. . . . Because every day, even when it's not the easy choice, we force ourselves not to put unnecessary limitations on her.

And I hope she never puts limitations on herself, either.

Roger Crawford smiles as he remembers what his father always used to say to him on the days that he was feeling embarrassed about his missing fingers or feeling sorry for himself or asking for a special extension on handwriting assignments: "You need to do the best you can with what you have. You're never going to be able to reach higher with your hands in your pockets."

# CHAPTER 23

## *More of the Same Than Different*

One day at a bus stop in 1998, a man named Rick Guidotti noticed a stunning young woman.

Her pale skin and white hair grabbed his attention, and he recognized her condition of albinism. Intrigued, Rick decided to learn more about albinism and began to research it through medical books and other resources available at this time before the age of Google.

But what he found was not what he expected: stark images in medical textbooks with black bars across the eyes. There were no stories, no people—only disease and diagnosis and medical terminology.

Rick was, interestingly enough, an esteemed fashion photographer at the time, shooting spreads and ads for *Elle*, *Vogue*, *GQ*, and many more. Seeing these types of medical images hugely contrasted the gorgeous images he created through his work with fashion models every day.

But, Rick believed, the people were no less beautiful. And so Rick Guidotti walked away from his fashion photography career to begin an organization called Positive Exposure.

Positive Exposure now utilizes photography and video to transform public perceptions of people living with genetic, physical, and behavioral differences—from albinism to autism to dwarfism to, yes, Brenna's condition of ichthyosis. His team has created educational and advocacy programs around the world to promote a more inclusive, compassionate world where differences are esteemed.

To see Rick in action is to feel a central part of this celebration. His energy is breathtaking, his upbeat attitude is contagious, and best of all, his subjects open up almost immediately to this energy and attitude with laughter and silly poses. Mothers have told Rick time and again, "My child is usually so shy and won't make eye contact with many people because they are so self-conscious of the way they look. I am amazed at how they were smiling for your camera."

Ultimately, Rick does what he does to promote the humanity in disability and difference. His motto is "Change how you see, see how you change."

One day, a woman Rick worked with told him that many people stare at her. . .but some turn away immediately to avoid eye contact, which can be even more painful than the stares.

"We need to steady that gaze," Rick realized, "long enough to see the beauty in difference, but also to see around the diversity to see what we all share—which is *humanity*."[28]

In being taught not to stare, sometimes we simply

28. Keynote speech, National Family Conference for the Foundation for Ichthyosis and Related Skin Types (Indianapolis, June 2014).

avoid. Because that is surely easier than looking but not looking too long, right?

Our eyes are a huge part of the way we communicate—the way we show we are listening, the way we signal to others without speaking, even a way to display how we feel.

Eye contact conveys a respect for the humanity of another.

When we avert our eyes, that communicates that we are embarrassed, that we don't wish to interact with some people. And though perhaps unintentionally, it may even suggest that we don't value them because of the way they look.

It happens every day. We see a woman in a wheelchair exiting through the automatic doors at the store. We glance over to a toddler who was born with several fingers missing. We notice a boy with a port-wine stain across his forehead. The time comes to pass by that person or hold the door open for him or her, and we look down or away. We don't want to stare, so we escape interaction altogether.

Yes, stares can be upsetting. But I tend to agree that avoiding is even worse. Stares and questions give us the opportunity to educate, or at least the opportunity to meet that person. If someone is staring, I meet his or her eyes and smile. And more often than not, I find that in meeting someone's eyes, that person has a chance to realize my daughter's humanity. That she is not just a "weird-looking kid". . .she has a mother who loves her. And that sometimes is worth more than anything I could say.

However, I've noticed a third look that is the most offensive: the glares.

There are stares, kids openmouthed, as they take in my daughter's reddened skin, flakes peeling on her arms and neck and face. There are awkward first, second, third glances. There are the people who pretend we don't exist.

And then there are the glares. The double takes from adults whose eyes narrow accusingly as they see Brenna's skin and shoot unseen daggers toward me when I glance their direction.

And I know what they are thinking without anyone needing to say a word: *How* could *you let your child get* sunburned *like that?*

Instead of judging my daughter, they judge me. They judge my parenting, my ability to care for my child. Because it is obvious to them that she is sunburned. All over her body. And the shiny covering? Aloe vera, surely.

Yes, the glares hurt the most. While I spend my days in a Groundhog Day–like cycle of moisturizing, exfoliating, bathing, and laundering—and trying not to be so overwhelmed by it all to keep me from mustering enough energy to be an attentive wife and mom who plays and reads and cooks, too—what those strangers see in that split second is an unfit mother.

Each time I catch one of those accusing glares, my heart aches a bit with anger and defensiveness. But even more than that and even better than that, it is a little reminder that we never know the whole story.

Global activist Stacey Edgar writes in her book *Global Girlfriend* about one of her former college professors whose favorite piece of career advice was "Where you stand depends on where you sit."

He was suggesting, Stacey remembers, that each of us needs to take the time to learn more about a person's history and experiences and feelings before we judge from our own personal throne.[29]

That one sentence from Stacey's professor is a strong reminder that we can never know exactly why people believe what they do, feel how they do, or make decisions the way they do (or let's not forget, *look* the way they do) without having experienced what those people have throughout their entire lives.

When we react based solely on how something appears, we've suddenly constructed a huge fence between ourselves and others. We've suddenly put ourselves in different categories—right and wrong, good and bad, beautiful and unattractive, better and not good enough. Without enough information or experience to even make that judgment, we're suddenly focused on the falsely conceived negativity

29. Stacey Edgar, *Global Girlfriend* (New York: St. Martin's, 2011), 17.

of our differences rather than our uniting sameness.

When Brenna was three and a half, someone asked me if Brenna wondered at all about why she looks different than most other kids. And at that age, that kind of question had never come up yet. I told the woman that our differing skin and appearances wasn't a typical topic of conversation in our house—not at all because it is taboo but rather because it isn't important. Brenna's appearance in our home has been a nonissue.

Actually, that very week, we had been spending the morning at a local library with such a fantastic children's section that it is often a preferred destination of many families in the area. A baby crawled up to Brenna as she stood next to the train table and stopped at Brenna's feet, intently watching her.

"Look!" Brenna exclaimed, pointing at the baby. "She has blue eyes like me!"

*Eyes like me.*

One of my all-time favorite books is *Same Kind of Different as Me*, which tells an incredible true story of the collision of several unlikely lives during events that are clearly orchestrated by God. Denver Moore is a black homeless man who has faced deep loss and poverty throughout his entire life. Ron Hall is a wealthy art dealer who is uncomfortable even driving by the homeless shelter. But Ron's wife, Debbie, who ultimately passes away after battling cancer, connects the two men, and their lives are forever changed, especially their faith.

By the end of the book, Denver—who was very resistant to Ron at first and took a long time to trust him—writes this profound statement:

> *I used to spend a lot of time worrying that I was different from other people, even from other homeless folks. Then after I met Miss Debbie and Mr. Ron, I worried that I was so different from them that we wasn't ever going to have no kind of future. But I found out that everybody's different—the same kind of different as me. We're all just regular folks walking down the road that God done set in front of us.*[30]

What we need to keep remembering while we learn to value our differences is that, when we are stripped to our basics, we are much more alike than we are different.

At the end of the day, our differences should make little difference in how we engage with each other, because our differences are not more important than our sameness. Our differences drive our uniqueness and our purpose, but our sameness is our humanity—we love the same and hurt the same.

As we strive to find appreciation for all the pieces of

30. Ron Hall, Denver Moore, and Lynn Vincent, *Same Kind of Different as Me* (Nashville: Thomas Nelson, 2006), 235.

our lives and our beliefs and our interests that set us apart from every single other person in the world, we need to also remember what we have in common: creation and love by the same God.

Making eye contact is one of the smallest and yet most important ways we can convey to those around us that we value them. "Steady our gaze," as Rick Guidotti says, to display respect, kindness, and understanding.

Maybe then we might actually see that the person across from us has "eyes like me."

# CHAPTER 24

## Telling Stories of Beauty with Our Lives

God gave our daughter a spitfire personality.

Brenna's doctors have long laughed about how "spunky" she is, and Evan needs to constantly remind me that her feisty personality is probably the reason she is alive today—usually as I'm counting down the seconds that stand between bedtime and a hot bubble bath.

As a toddler and preschooler, Brenna fights me on so many things: what particular shoes or dress she wants to wear, which stroller she wants to ride in, what she does or doesn't want to eat (dinnertime is an absolute *treat* some nights). This morning, her shrieks erupted because she wanted pepperoni for a snack, not the summer sausage that was already cut up and packed, and she wanted to wear her blue jacket, not her yellow one—even though it's chilly and her yellow one is warmer—and she insisted that she likes being cold, which is an outright lie.

How much easier would it be to just give in to her demands and keep the calm? Yet, I push her back. Not only because she needs to learn obedience and reasoning and compromise, but also because this daughter of mine will likely be put in many confrontational situations over the course of her life regarding her skin. If the past few years are any indication, she will be asked over and over—in some not very nice ways—about her appearance. She will be offered remedies or given medical advice from strangers who know very little about her or her condition. And she may very well be treated "differently," in all kinds of ways—pitied, scorned, avoided.

I want Brenna to learn how to choose her battles wisely. I need her to know that how she treats others does not have to be a reflection of how she is treated.

Because if everything becomes a raging fight every day, then we begin to tell a story with our lives of struggle, of defensiveness, and of victimization.

We are storytellers with this one life we have been given. We are the main characters in this incredible story, and even when we don't realize it, God is weaving through our story and using our story to impact the world around us.

With every choice we make, we get to choose how to tell this story of our lives. We may not always have control over what happens to us, but we choose how to react to these experiences, and through that, we decide on the genre of our story. Will we be the hero or the victim? Will we write for ourselves a beautiful story worth reading and sharing?

As author Shauna Niequist describes in her book *Cold*

*Tangerines*, it takes a kind of courage to choose the genre of your own story:

> *When you realize that the story of your life could be told a thousand different ways, that you could tell it over and over as a tragedy, but you choose to call it an epic, that's when you start to learn what celebration is.*
>
> *When what you see in front of you is so far outside of what you dreamed, but you have the belief, the boldness, the courage to call it beautiful instead of calling it wrong, that's celebration.[31]*

When you are the author of your own life, you get to decide what makes it into your story—what defines you and drives you and paints the scenes of your existence. And through your actions and your reactions, you also get to decide what scenes don't make the cut.

During the summer of 2015, my aunts, uncles, and cousins began talking about doing a big family trip together—to a water-park resort.

My heart sank a bit when I thought about taking Brenna to a water park in the hot July weather. The water would be too cold, the air would be too hot, and germs would be everywhere. *Everywhere.*

And most of all, there would be a whole lot of kids and

31. Shauna Niequist, *Cold Tangerines* (Grand Rapids: Zondervan, 2007), 178.

adults. . .people who probably had never seen a child with her condition and who would surely stare, judge, perhaps even ridicule or comment.

We ultimately agreed to go. And our kids talked excitedly about that trip for weeks in advance.

God must have granted favor upon that water-park weekend, because the weather was perfect for Brenna. She was able to be outside almost the entire time with no fear of overheating. She was thrilled with trying a tiny slide or two, but she was just as thrilled being a part of the fun, watching the big kids race and ride their tube slides. Oh, and she had a new swimsuit, so she strutted about in her latest fashions.

That's all I talked about when we got home—how great it was. We had fantastic weather, she didn't get sick, we were able to properly care for her skin, and our family time was invaluable.

My fears about stares were not unfounded. Kids would stop and stare openmouthed at her, adults would turn around to continue looking at her, and a group of high school kids pointed and gawked. I read their lips as they exclaimed, "Oh my *gosh*!"

But those stares—those are not part of our story. Those encounters were not what I chose to include in my story as I raved about our weekend on my blog and to my friends. Our story is so much better than that, and we chose to celebrate the wonderful of the weekend, not the negative.

We can choose to tell our stories however we want.

It is stepping onto the path of courage that allows us to actually focus on the good over the bad. Anyone can complain. Anyone can feel self-pity.

But it takes a certain boldness to stand up and tell a story of celebration. It takes courage to push aside the negative and write our own story of triumph—not just once, but again and again. Choosing this path of courage day after day leads to a life of wonder and beauty, joy and accomplishment—not only in telling our story but in living it out.

As Austin Kleon writes in his book *Steal Like an Artist*: "Write the kind of story you like best—write the story you want to read. Whenever you're at a loss for what move to make next, just ask yourself, 'What would make a better story?' "[32]

Through blogging and writing, I came to know a woman and fellow mom named Sarah Kovac. Sarah was born with a congenital birth defect that left her with barely useable arms, and she has worked over her life to use her feet as hands.

When she was younger, Sarah went through seasons of unhappiness and depression, just wanting to be like the pretty and popular girls in her class. She felt the loss of

---

32. Austin Kleon, *Steal Like an Artist* (New York: Workman, 2012), 47.

being "shortchanged" as she struggled to understand why her arms didn't work the way others' arms did, and she sank more and more into her unhappiness, blaming every problem or negative emotion on her disability.

But eventually, Sarah realized that she had more control over the way she felt than she originally believed.

"As I spent all my mental energy finding creative ways to dump all my sorrows on my disability, I relieved myself of the responsibility to change," she writes in her book, *In Capable Arms*. "That I believed my unhappiness to be out of my control further contributed to my unhappiness."[33]

Sarah begin to discover that she could write her own story in life, both despite and because of the body she'd been given. Though perhaps not as easy a route as wallowing in pity and blaming everything else around her, Sarah started to write a new story for herself.

*Sometimes we fool ourselves into believing that we aren't doing anything to perpetuate painful circumstances. It's more comfortable to believe we are just the victims and there's not a thing we can do. . .how we react determines whether we're really a victim or whether we allow our experiences to make us better. I need to grieve my pain, but I don't have to be a victim.*[34]

33. Sarah Kovac, *In Capable Arms* (Nashville, TN: Abingdon, 2013), 70.
34. Kovac, *In Capable Arms*, 71–72.

Sarah met her wonderful husband and eventually had two children—a son and a daughter—and every day, she accomplishes simple motherhood tasks like changing a diaper or preparing dinner with her feet. She wrote a new story for herself, one of love and perseverance and self-appreciation, and she shares her story now as beautiful, not as a victim of misfortune.

We hear the word *wrong* a lot as it pertains to our daughter.

"What's wrong with her face?"

"What's wrong with her skin?"

"What's *wrong* with *her*?"

I know what they are referring to. But to be honest, I really don't know what they actually mean.

Because there is ultimately nothing wrong with Brenna. There is nothing wrong about her, nothing that is bad or a mistake. I don't believe that our awesome God is capable of mistakes.

We could easily decide to tell her story as a tragedy. We could choose to focus on her limits, to live in fear of hospitalizations or sickness, to feel sorry for her, to be angry at her condition and its effect on her life.

Our great Creator weaves the stories of our lives together and intersects them with others' stories, and it is up to us how we choose to tell that story.

Since the time of Brenna's birth, God has been working

through me, giving me the courage to stand up and say that my daughter is not wrong—she is beautiful. We believe wholeheartedly that Brenna was given to us uniquely and beautifully created by God, not that she was given to us broken.

Living out and sharing our beautiful stories every day—both the failures and the successes—reveals the incredible ways God is moving in our lives. When we step up to share this with others, we are sharing God's love and sovereignty with them.

May we choose to create and to tell dazzling stories of beauty with our lives, through our thoughts, actions, and reactions. May we choose our battles wisely so that we can tell stories not of anger or victimization but of grace, courage, and acceptance of self and others. Stories of intense purpose, not of wrongness.

We are different, and we are the same—none of us is perfect, but we were formed purposely by a perfect Creator. That is not wrong; that's a story worth living and worth telling.

# CHAPTER 25

## The Cycle of Celebrating Beautiful

Last year, Brenna and I arrived home from the library, about to cozy up with one of our newly borrowed reads, when I took a quick bathroom break. And as I pushed the door open and stepped into our main-level bathroom, my bare foot was seeped in water.

I flipped the light on to reveal a bathroom soaking wet. Water covered the toilet and the sink, with puddles all over the floor. I quickly ran downstairs to our unfinished basement to find a small pool of water on the cement floor there as well.

And then, after dashing up to our second floor, I was met with standing water in the hallway. The carpet squished with my steps in the nearby bedrooms, and water pooled in Brenna's bathroom. Finally, in the laundry room filled with more puddles, we found the culprit: the hose on the back of the washing machine had come loose from the drain-pipe and drained a whole load all over our home.

Within an hour or two, we had a restoration team at the house, placing huge, roaring fans throughout and tearing up flooring that we had installed just one year before when we moved in.

This incident came directly on the heels of a night spent in the playroom with the whole family after our air-conditioning upstairs had broken—an adventure for the kids, and a sleepless, uncomfortable night for me and Evan. Also that week, we had discovered that during Brenna's eight-day hospitalization the previous month, she had contracted a skin infection, and she had passed it on to me and to Connor. It was not my favorite week, to say the least.

But over the noise of the fans and the workers tearing up my house, my heart had an overwhelming emotion: gratitude.

To be honest, I surprised myself with these feelings of thanks, because my overriding personality would typically be extremely stressed. But all I kept thinking was that it could have been so much worse. The damage could have been much more extensive had we not found it and begun cleaning it so early, and it could have affected things like electronics (my computer—shudder) or much-less-easy-to-replace items like photo albums.

Insurance would cover most of the repairs. We could afford our deductible because of an emergency savings account.

And above all, this was merely a headache. An inconvenience. A fixable problem.

As I felt this gratitude swirl in me, I realized that my heart was coming full circle.

Ever since Brenna's birth shook up everything we thought we knew, God had been reshaping and remolding my heart to discover all the joy and the beauty that this new world was trying to offer us. I opened myself up to this transformation as I faced each new trial and each new triumph. . .seeking, begging, learning, and finding strength, peace, gratitude, and joy.

As we seek, we find. As we ask, we receive. And as we choose, we allow within us.

By deliberately seeking joy and choosing joy throughout the challenges and the sickness, I realized that I had begun to find joy even when I wasn't intentionally looking for it. By seeking to praise God and choosing to praise God within the trials and uncertainty of life, I had begun to find gratitude even when I wasn't intentionally reaching for it.

With a heart filled with joy over anger, peace over anguish, strength over despair, we can then begin to experience a full appreciation for so much of God's beauty that we may never have considered before. We can build a life of contentment and gratitude as we appreciate and celebrate this different beautiful.

Beautiful has very little to do with appearance—or at least as it pertains to hair color and noses and shoes.

Beautiful is a way of *being* and a way of *living*, each and every day, perhaps each and every moment.

Beautiful is joy radiating from your soul.

Beautiful can be found *everywhere*, when we take the time to see it, when we *want* to see it. Beautiful can be wherever we seek it—in motherhood, in our homes, in our children, in marriage, in ourselves, in our faith, in our emotions, and in our experiences.

The world, through God, is giving us all kinds of beautiful. It's time for us to be brave. It's time for us to take this different beautiful as it is offered to us and allow it to change us, to make us better, to connect us with others.

If we're going to open our hearts and live a life that celebrates a different beautiful, we need to shake off the unrealistic expectations, unwritten rules, and false definitions of normal that we place upon ourselves or allow others to pile on us. Living a life according to God's definition of beautiful means ignoring the should-bes and, instead, chasing the could-bes.

So what now? What is next?

Think about the people you find the most beautiful.

When asked about the most beautiful person you know, whom do you describe? Your mom. Your spouse. Your best friend. Your children. The people you *love*.

We find the people we love the most beautiful beings in our lives because of the joy they bring to our lives and the way they make us *feel*. Their beauty is in their living and in their being and in their doing—not in the way their noses are shaped or how long their legs are.

Think about the times that you feel the most beautiful.

Not when you necessarily think you *look* the most beautiful, but when you truly, actually *feel* it. The moments that you are living in joy, that you are seeking and finding the exquisite beautiful of the small moments, that you are surprised by a dazzling moment of beauty in the unexpected. The moments when you choose to let Jesus' light shine through you.

If we want to see a change in how people view each other, it starts with us. If we want our children to grow up learning to appreciate differences and learning how to see God's version of beautiful in this life, instead of our pop culture's version, it starts with us. Teaching them by showing them is an incredible gift we can give our children.

More times than I can count, I have been thrilled when a family has approached us who has recognized us from social media, wanting to say hello. . .only to be dismayed when that family's children stand back and furrow their brows at Brenna's appearance. It is clear that although the mother has apparently enjoyed reading about our daughter and seeing our family's photos online, she never took the time to share with her children. Often mothers will share with me how Brenna's story has helped changed their perspective regarding special-needs parenting and differences, but then, it is obvious by the confused reactions of their kids that they haven't yet thought to pass those lessons on to their children.

If we allow stories and experiences to inspire us for a moment, or even to begin changing our hearts, but we don't take the time to show our children and teach our children about these new perspectives, we are missing the point. If it starts and stops with us, we will never see real and lasting change in the hearts of those around us and in the way our children see themselves and treat others.

It is not enough to simply be inspired. It is not enough to simply desire for your children to be kind and accepting. It is not even enough to allow God to work within your heart and your life, from the inside out. We need to use that transformation within our hearts to lead us to action. To share about the different beautiful that is touching and impacting our lives. To tell our stories about the way God is offering splendor in our lives in all kinds of ways so that others may experience this different beautiful. To be kind—offering help to those who need it, meeting the eyes of those we encounter with respect, offering grace before we become defensive, and realizing we don't know the whole story because we are quick to judge.

And perhaps most importantly, taking this change in our hearts and this new appreciation for different kinds of dazzling beauty and passing it on to our children—teaching them through all kinds of experiences what kindness looks like, teaching them what it really means to appreciate and celebrate people for who they are and the uniqueness they bring and the parts of the puzzle that they fill.

What an extraordinary impact this will have in the classroom, on the bus, on the sports field, in the band room, and around the dinner table. What a changed dynamic will naturally occur in our relationships because of the gratitude and contentment developed and cultivated out of this appreciation and celebration.

That is not to say that each moment has to be seized in a full carpe diem of happiness and cheer despite all else— because it won't be but rather that we allow contentment and kindness to overtake our hearts and to fill up our souls and to filter into our everyday actions and relationships, instead of jealousy, insecurity, or negativity.

Learning to appreciate the unexpected leaves you without feelings of disappointment at every sharp turn of the path. Learning to embrace differences that others have to offer, through their interests, passions, and appearances, removes the desire to compare, removes the fear that breeds prejudice.

It's been interesting for me, year after year of raising Brenna, to see how we as a culture automatically believe that someone who has physical differences or is disabled in any way is wrong or bad. It's time to stop perpetuating this idea that these differences should be ostracized instead of embraced and glorified.

For our family, we now know a different beautiful, a beautiful that the world might struggle to see or understand, but those of us who know and love Brenna have gratefully been given the gift of understanding this different beautiful.

This kind of transformation comes from the personal choices we make in our lives. Every time we decide to write our story as one that is positive and good, every time we turn a setback into a comeback, every time we choose to praise and be grateful even in the hard, and every time we meet another person's eyes with kindness, that's when we are learning how to truly live a life of celebration.

Discovering a different beautiful in our lives is a mind-set we practice with each experience and person we meet and connect with, but for full transformation, it comes from a change—sometimes a very gradual change—within our hearts, as we allow God to work in us and through us. . .from the inside out.

# ACKNOWLEDGMENTS:

I always read every acknowledgments page when I come to the end of books, and I've long since dreamed about what I might write if I got the chance to publish a book. But when the time came, I realized how difficult this proved, because of what a tremendous community it takes to support a writing journey. Simply typing "thank you" feels so insufficient, so I hope you all know how deep my gratitude runs—not only for bringing this book to life but bringing *me* to life every day with your ongoing love and encouragement.

To my husband, Evan, I want to thank you for always believing in me. For being the logic to my enthusiastic and well-meaning insanity. You pick me up where I leave off. You make me laugh more than anyone. Who would have known that smiling at the cute blue-eyed boy in the hall at Farm-House would lead to nine love-filled years of marriage? I'm deeply grateful for your unending devotion to our family.

Connor, I am so proud to be your mother, and I am so delighted in the extraordinary person I see growing before my eyes. God knew just what he was doing when he gave you to us as our son and Brenna's older brother—you are so special to our family.

Brenna, what a glorious creation you are—made in the unique image of our loving God. Every day, I am amazed to bear witness to your spunk, determination, and beauty. I am so glad you came along to complete our family.

To my parents, I am so grateful for all of the sacrifices you made to help me get where I am and mold me into the woman I am today. For always being my biggest fans, for all of the encouragement you have given, time you have devoted and listening hours you have offered, and for teaching me what compassion and unconditional love truly mean—*thank you*. I love you so much.

A very special thanks to my agent, Blythe Daniel, for believing in my story from the moment we met and for guiding me so expertly throughout this entire process. I am honored not only to get to work with such a gifted and grace-filled agent, but also to be able to call you a dear friend.

To Kelly, Shalyn, and my entire publishing team at Barbour, I offer my thanks and tremendous appreciation for championing this project and giving it your passionate support. Thank you for listening, for helping to mold my ideas into something wonderful, and for taking to heart the message of this book and helping to share it across the world.

I also want to thank:

My in-laws, Bill and Jeannine, for raising such a wonderful son and being such devoted grandparents to our children.

My amazingly supportive group of family members and friends, for everything you have done for me and for our family throughout all walks of my life. I can't even begin to name you all, but you know who you are.

My blog readers, who have adopted our family as your own and who have opened your hearts to joining us in discovering this different beautiful.

And finally, my eternal gratitude for our Great God—I am so humbled by Your presence in my life, by Your forgiveness, and by Your sovereignty. I am deeply                                                                                      for
Your                                                                                            ost
wond

Cou                                                                                         l,
Evar                                                                                       s
born                                                                                       n
ichtl                                                                                      e
and                                                                                        l
speci                                                                                      s
such                                                                                       ,
and                                                                                        s
phot